Arnold White

The Destitute Alien in Great Britain

A Series of Papers Dealing with the Subject of Foreign Pauper Immigration

Arnold White

The Destitute Alien in Great Britain
A Series of Papers Dealing with the Subject of Foreign Pauper Immigration

ISBN/EAN: 9783337031077

Printed in Europe, USA, Canada, Australia, Japan

Cover: Foto ©Suzi / pixelio.de

More available books at **www.hansebooks.com**

THE DESTITUTE ALIEN

IN

GREAT BRITAIN

A Series of Papers Dealing with the Subject of
Foreign Pauper Immigration

ARRANGED AND EDITED BY
ARNOLD WHITE

London
SWAN SONNENSCHEIN & CO.
NEW YORK: CHARLES SCRIBNER'S SONS
1892

A FUTURE volume will deal with the economical bearing, American example, and medical and sanitary aspect of Free Immigration; also with the Jewish question and recent events in Russia.

Illness and compulsory absence from England have rendered it impossible for me to complete the arrangements for bringing out the work as a whole within the limits of time prescribed by expediency.

I have to thank my friend Mr. C. B. Shaw for his good offices in seeing this volume through the press.

A. W.

CONTENTS.

THE
DESTITUTE ALIEN IN GREAT BRITAIN

INTRODUCTORY.

BY ARNOLD WHITE.

THE growth of population and the pressure of existence
within these islands have occasioned, for some considerable time past, anxiety on the part of those in
search of remedies for the evil conditions under which
so many of our fellow-subjects are compelled to toil.
Among the causes that have not yet received adequate
and dispassionate examination, is the flow of foreign
labour to our great towns, with its moral, physical,
and economical effects on the native population.
Throughout the civilized, and in parts of the un-
civilized world, a strange movement is taking place
towards the crystallization of national life from native
elements only, and the rejection of those alien con-
stituents which, since the fall of Rome, have generally
been considered desirable for the creation of perfect
national existence. This movement is no less marked
in the United States of America than in Russia,
or even in Arabia itself. The increased and increasing
stringency of the conditions under which Castle

B

Garden permits the entry of the Irish, Hungarian or Italian proletariat, finds a parallel in the renaissance of orthodoxy in Russia. The disfavour into which heterodox faiths have there fallen, under the iron hand and strong convictions of the Attorney-General of the Holy Synod, and the consequent alliance of those forces of ignorance and of strength that have hitherto occupied a dominant position in the history of modern Russia, are producing much the same effects as the anti-alienism of the United States. In Mahommedan countries too, this note of national revival is no less dominant than in lands where faith is less effectual to stir the harmonies of nationalism than self-interest, as in the case of the United States; ambition, as in France; or the memory of a glorious but vanished past, as in Portugal. Arabia, and a large part of Central Africa, have recently become the scene of a violent insurrection against the foreign element, and a consequent drawing nigh of those who hold undimmed the original doctrine of Mohammed.

England, thanks to the Huguenots, Mr. Cobden, the Slave Trade, the Jews, and an inherent capacity for taking large views of grave national questions, has been the last country in all the world to question, or even to examine, the doctrine that uninterrupted ingress for men, women, and merchandise of other nations, is essential to and advantageous to her national life. There are, however, no longer wanting

signs that the reign of this dogma is not to continue
without challenge. Two phenomena combine to render
a critical examination of the effects of the doctrine
of free entry of all human beings not only inevitable
but indispensable. The first of these phenomena
is the attitude of the citizens of the United States
towards the whole subject of immigration, and the
other is, the revival in Russia of the Middle-Age
methods of dealing with the Jewish question. The
first of these phenomena has set men thinking how
far a policy of free immigration that is bad for the
United States, with its vast and but partially occupied
territory, can be good for the United Kingdom with
its daily increasing population and diminishing capacity for the production of its own food. The second is
the recent Russian practice of harrying the poor Jews
until they fly their country in sheer despair, thus
creating a centrifugal force for the distribution of
needy and unskilled workers, which has already
affected Great Britain, and cannot fail to affect her
in the future to a still greater extent.

So far as Great Britain is concerned, the question
is unlikely to be settled without a more thorough
examination into the facts than has yet been made.
The House of Commons Committee on Immigration
touched but the fringe of the subject, and seemed
more interested in demonstrating that those who
wished to restrict and regulate immigration desired

to attack the civil and religious liberty now happily accorded to the Jews, than in bringing out the true physical, moral and economical results of the system as now followed in England.

The Sweating Committee of the House of Lords refused to accept direct evidence bearing on the subject, for fear of trenching on the rights and privileges of the Commons Committee, which was concurrently occupied in the ostensible examination of the immigration question. The consequence is that while the country thinks the subject has been fairly considered, nothing has taken place but a fruitless wrangle on the Jewish question, which has nothing whatever to do with the matter.

Accordingly, it is my intention to endeavour to place before the public practical information provided by experts on the various points from which the whole subject may be regarded. The present volume is but an instalment of the whole work.

THE HUGUENOT AND FLEMISH INVASION.

By C. B. Shaw.

THE discovery of printing, with the impulse thereby given to religious and political thought, although in the end of incalculable advantage to mankind, was, by strange contrast with the blessings it conferred, a principal factor in the persecutions inflicted on the Protestants throughout Europe in the sixteenth and seventeenth centuries.

During the long night of the middle ages science and letters had fallen into decay, and the Church, far from struggling against the mental darkness prevailing, had done its best to maintain it. The austere and penitential devotions of the early Christians had been gradually succeeded by perverted doctrines, sacerdotal tyranny, and ceremonials strangely allied to pagan rites; and while the mass of the people were the slaves of the Church in mind and body, the clergy themselves were so degraded that purity of manners and ecclesiastical rules were alike disregarded. A large proportion of the land was in the hands of the Church, exempt from any corresponding duty or obligation to the State; yet so

5

insatiable was the greed of that Sacred Institution
that it would soon have absorbed the whole wealth of
Europe had not the secular governments interposed.
In the pulpit preachers confined their exhortations
to alms-giving, pilgrimages, and the obtaining of
religious indulgences, the traffic in the latter being
carried to such a pitch that papal pardons were sold
in parts of Christendom openly in the streets and to
the sound of the drum. Seminaries of learning, widely
scattered, and manuscripts, costly and difficult to
obtain, were the only resources of literary culture;
the voices of the few pious and enlightened souls
who laboured for letters in the retirement of cloister
or study being inaudible to the masses for want of
proper channels of communication. False traditions
in history, amazing superstitions in religion, universal
belief in astrology, and barbarous punishment for
heresy — even for offences against the Church un-
intentionally committed—marked the degradation of
the age.

Such, then, was the condition of France—which, like
the rest of Europe, had lain for centuries mute and
despairing before the impassable barrier of bigotry
and ignorance—when the wooden blocks of Laurence
Coster, and the metal types of Gutenberg and his
fellow workmen, proclaimed to the world, at first in
the reserved and doubtful language of experiment,
but finally in the bold and confident voice of assured

success, the dawn of modern liberty and the emancipation of the human mind.

The efforts of the printers were at first slow and laborious, the Mazarin Bible taking some seven or eight years to finish; but copies of the Scriptures and ancient authors were in course of time widely distributed and eagerly read. Luther, Zwingle, and other ardent spirits began to preach the doctrines of the Reformation, including the Supremacy of the Written Word—now brought within the reach of all, and the Church of Rome, jealous of the new crusade, commenced its onslaught against preachers, printers, and books alike.

In spite, however, of persecutions and prohibitions, books multiplied, and the reformers gained numberless converts. The ranks of the Lutherans were swelled not merely by the poor and lowly, but members of princely houses, nobles, priests, and earnest supporters of the Catholic hierarchy rallied to their standard.

So electrical were the effects of the religious reform, that at length the very foundations of the Papacy began to totter. The more politic men of the day, alive to the signs of the approaching storm, tried to allay it by recalling the Church to a sense of its own position, and by urging the introduction of timely reforms; but without avail. The Holy See, either from stupidity or incorrigible pride, turned a deaf ear to the counsel of its friends, and betook itself to those measures which were soon to make its name a terror and a reproach to humanity.

Meaux, from its proximity to the then Flemish frontier, and other circumstances that favoured the transmission of influences from the north, was the first town in France to respond to the new movement. Guillaume Briçonnet, the Bishop of the Meaux, joined heartily in it, and by offering the pulpits of his absentee clergy to Lefevre, Farel, and other disciples of Luther, and distributing copies of the Bible among the workshops, soon made his diocese a centre of dissent. Other places followed the lead of Meaux, and as the conversions spread, attendances at mass naturally fell off and Church revenues declined. The Sorbonne—the Faculty of Theology at Paris, and the inspiring author of many a cruel edict—thereupon petitioned Parliament to interpose its authority, with the result that partisans of the pernicious doctrines were persecuted wherever found, those who were unable to save themselves by flight being burnt alive. The execution of the Placardists and the butchery of the Vaudois were further instances of the Church's "discipline;" but towards the end of the reign of Francis I., says De Félice, "the movement had made such extended strides that it was impossible to follow its course in all its windings . . . there was in the minds and hearts of men, even in the air they breathed, an overwhelming desire for religious reform."

The term " Huguenot," whatever its origin, soon became the distinctive appellation of the advocates of the new propaganda, who, for the next hundred years at least, were destined to play so important a part in French history. The elements of order were introduced into their hitherto defective organization, and Calvin took the place of Luther as the apostle of French Protestantism.

Within the limits prescribed me it is only possible briefly to sketch the chain of circumstances that eventually led to the exodus of the French Protestants. No impartial writer, however, can touch upon the history of that period without observing that in the course of their bitter struggle, they were moved by political as well as by religious considerations. Many men of great influence, who were disaffected towards the Government, or jealous of the court faction, joined the Huguenots in the hope of furthering political aims; indeed, so numerous and important were the accessions to their ranks, from one cause and another, that for a time it looked as if the supreme authority were likely to fall into their hands—a fact which goes far to explain, although it does not excuse, the part played both by Church and State in the measures adopted to destroy them.

The royal decree of 1562, guaranteeing liberty of

worship to Protestants, having been openly set at defiance by the Catholics, and the massacre of Vassy, followed by the destruction of Protestant Churches, having provoked reprisals, France became for a time the theatre of civil war.

Sheer exhaustion on both sides at length brought the conflict to an end, and the treaty of St. Germains was signed; but the peace proved of short duration. The Queen Mother, Catherine de Medecis, laying aside her temporizing policy, now went entirely over to the Guise party, and, with the assistance of foreign counsellors, fresh schemes were devised for the extirpation of heretics. The marriage of Henry of Navarre became the occasion of the treacherous assassination of Admiral Coligny and the oft-recounted Massacre of Saint Bartholomew. For four days the streets of Paris ran with the blood of those who were bidden to Catherine's hideous *festa*. But this was not enough: the provinces also were made to contribute their share to the blood-offering; for six weeks similar scenes were enacted throughout the length and breadth of France, and a hundred thousand Huguenots paid the penalty of heresy. To commemorate the event a medal was struck, which bore the strange device, "Piety has awakened justice."

The wars of the League which followed these barbarous acts were only terminated on the accession of Henry of Navarre to the throne, and in 1598 the pro-

mulgation of the Edict of Nantes once more accorded
to Protestants liberty of conscience and of worship.
The freedom they enjoyed was, however, but short-
lived; for, on the assassination of the king, religious
discord again broke loose, and for years the Huguenots
were the victims of ever varying acts of persecution.

After the siege of Rochelle, where the English
twice ignominiously failed to relieve their Protestant
allies, the Huguenots ceased to exist as an armed
force or a political party. Being treated in a more
tolerant spirit by Cardinals Richelieu and Mazarin,
they showed a wise discretion, stood resolutely
aloof from civil broils, and if they took up arms at
all, it was, as has been acknowledged, almost invariably on the side of loyalty. Colbert, the enlightened minister of Louis XIV., also protected them as
far as he dared; and, although during his lifetime
they were subject to disabilities and indignities against
which he frequently protested, it was not till after his
death, and mainly under the evil influences of the
triumvirate consisting of Père la Chaise, Prime
Minister Louvois, and Madame de Maintenon, that
those persecutions were renewed which crushed them
in countless numbers, and denuded France of the
flower of her population.

Had the Huguenots been treated with leniency
they would have remained loyal and industrious
subjects of the crown, and France would not have

had occasion to bewail the loss to her commerce, industries, and wealth, to which their dispersion condemned her. But the persecutions directed against them after the revocation of the Edict of Nantes, in 1685, passed the bounds of human endurance. Prohibition of all forms of Protestant worship, destruction of churches, abduction of children, wholesale conversions at the point of the sword, dragonnades which spared neither sex nor age, dungeons for the men, convent prisons for the women, every means that subtlety could devise or tyranny carry out, were adopted by the "Great Monarch" and his Christian agents to stamp out heresy and make France the untainted rival of Catholic Spain.

Before the Revocation, Colbert cautioned Louis against the effects of his insane policy. "I am sorry to say it," he observed, "but too many of your Majesty's subjects are already among your neighbours as footmen and valets for their daily bread; many of the artisans, too, are fled from the severity of your collectors, and are at this time improving the manufactures of your enemies"—the English to wit.

Penalties were now enacted, against which "conversion" was the only door of escape to those who wished to remain in France; but the spirit of the Huguenot rebelled against so mean an evasion. He would suffer death, or serve in the galleys, he would leave his kindred, his wealth, even the country of his birth — which to a Frenchman has ever been the symbol of his adoration, his devout conception of God's choicest work—all these he would renounce with manly resignation, but betray his conscience he would not.

It was the same in Flanders. Causes similar to those that brought about the flight of the Huguenots, and which are fully described in the brilliant pages of Motley, induced the Flemings who professed the Protestant faith to leave their country and seek in Holland, Germany and England that liberty of worship and personal freedom which were denied them at home. The Church of Rome, acting in concert with the civil rulers, had adopted the same infamous processes against the Protestants in the Flemish dominions of Philip II. (with the added terrors of the Holy Inquisition) as characterized the persecution of the Reformed Church in France; and the results were in the two countries almost identical. Antwerp, which is said to have done more business in one month than Venice in two years when at the very height of her grandeur, became deserted; Bruges and Ghent, abandoned by their respectable citizens, Catholic as well as Protestant, became crowded with thieves and paupers, and the whole trade of Flanders was ruined. As in the case of the Huguenots the Flemish Protestants carried to the countries which gave them asylum, England among the number, the skill, the intelligence and the industry that had made their own country rich and prosperous.

Whilst the capitulation of Rochelle sealed the fate of the Huguenots as a political party, the Revocation of the Edict of Nantes put an end to such vestiges of religious freedom as the dragoons of Louis XIV., and the tender regard of the Jesuits for their spiritual welfare, had failed to confiscate. Many men of distinction fled to Holland, among others Jurieu, the professor of Hebrew and Theology at the Protestant University of Sedan, and Huyghens, the Astronomer and Mathematician. Some few, for the sake of services rendered to their country, were exceptionally favoured by being freely permitted to leave it and settle elsewhere. Among these were Marshal Schomberg, a man of distinguished family and high military capacity, who subsequently served under William, Prince of Orange, and was killed at the battle of the Boyne, also the Marquis de Ruvigny, whose son entered the English service and became Earl of Galway. Admiral Duquesne, "the first sailor in France," was, in consequence of his great age, allowed to end his days in his native country. His two sons went to Holland.

But means of escape became daily more difficult. The sea-coast and inland frontiers were jealously guarded, and those who were captured by the king's scouts were treated with the utmost barbarity. The men, old and young, were condemned to instant death, or to the galleys for life. Servants who aided and abetted the escape of their masters were flogged and branded with the fleur-de-lis, the emblem of French Sovereignty; magistrates, merchants, pastors, peasants, all alike were forced to make long marches, sometimes in chains, and in the company of thieves and cut-throats, and were urged along, did they but falter by the way, with blows and imprecations; women were torn from their husbands, and children from their mothers' breasts. It is a relief to read that in many instances the priests themselves revolted against the unnecessary cruelties the Protestants were made to suffer, and endeavoured to assuage their lot. The women, even those who had been bred in luxury and refinement, faced hardship, and resorted to every conceivable disguise in attempting to escape. They cut off their hair, disfigured their faces with juices and dyes that coloured and blistered their skins, dressed themselves like men, assumed the character of lackeys or peasants, drew wheel-barrows, carried manure, walked hundreds of miles through snow and mud, enduring with unmurmuring fortitude hunger and thirst, every imaginable priva-tion, rather than abjure their faith or submit to the tyranny of their oppressors. Those who were dis-covered and arrested were thrown into prison or immured in convents. Persons of gentle birth,

pregnant women, old men, children and invalids,
many who had never seen the sea before, braved its
perils, and entrusted themselves in open boats in
their eagerness to escape. They fled in French,
English and Dutch merchant vessels, hidden under
bales of goods, heaps of coals, and in empty casks.
Other instances might be mentioned of courage and
fortitude, of dangers faced and hardships undergone
by Protestants of both sexes and all ages in their
efforts to escape rather than endure the ignominy of
conversion, or the debasing terms on which immunity from persecution was to be purchased; but
enough has been said to show the spirit of our foreign
settlers.

That the Huguenots were loyal when treated with
clemency is shown by their conduct during the wars
of the Fronde, by their refusal to assist the Duke of
Montmorency in his endeavour to excite rebellion in
Languedoc, and by their action at Rochelle when they
supported the Regent against their own governor.
Louis XIV., too, had actually thanked them at the
beginning of his reign "for the consistent manner
in which they had supported the royal authority."
That they were laborious, honest and enterprising is
shown by the condition of France before and after
their flight. Louis Blanc says of them that "they
made France an industrial power," and that the term
Protestant was "synonymous with wealth." To be

"honest as a Huguenot," moreover, became a pro-
verb. Being excluded from civil and political offices
on account of their religion, the Huguenots had
devoted themselves to industrial pursuits, and were
the best farmers, wine-growers, merchants and manufacturers in France. The heaviest crops were to be
found on Huguenot farms, the finest woollen cloth
was of their manufacture, and so, also, were many
other articles largely exported to England and
Holland. Their paper mills were the best in Europe,
and the steel and iron industries of Sedan were known
far and wide. "If the Nîmes merchants are bad
Catholics, at any rate they have not ceased to be good
traders," once wrote one of their bitterest persecutors.
Smiles attributes much of their success in business
to the fact that their time was less broken into by
feast and fast days than in the case of the Catholics,
and that they were therefore able to work more con-
tinuously. It is probable that the training of their
schools, some of which had obtained a European reputation, contributed materially to their acknowledged
superiority in most walks of life. The recognised
fairness and ability displayed in their business dealings, also gave them to an enormous extent the
command of foreign trade; the great centres of
French commerce, such as Bordeaux, Rouen and
Caen, being almost entirely governed by Huguenot
merchants. Jurieu, writing on the subject, remarked

c

that "the Protestants have carried commerce with
them into exile;" and the Catholic merchants of
Metz also complained that "it was impossible to
recover the connection with foreign markets which
the flight of the most considerable traders of the
town had broken." Poole quotes several instances,
both from the point of view of population and trade,
as typical of the injury resulting from the flight of
the Protestants. He observes, "that Lyons, which
had employed 18,000 silk looms, had but 4,000 remaining at the end of the century. Tours, with the same
interest, had had 800 mills, 80,000 looms and 40,000
workpeople, and in 1727, only 70 mills, 1,200 looms
and perhaps 4,000 workpeople. Of its 3,000 ribbon-
factories only 60 remained. Equally significant was
the ruin of the woollen trade of Poitou, the drugget
manufactures of Coulonges, the serge and bombazine
manufactures of Thouars and Châtaigneraie, and the
export trade to Canada, by way of Rochelle." Normandy, Brittany, Picardy, Burgundy, Lorraine, Languedoc, every part of France which had prospered
owing to the sterling character and incessant industry
of its Protestant inhabitants, felt the paralysing effects
of the general exodus, and it required all the efforts of
her subsequent rulers, all the fertility of her soil, all the
resource and versatility of her sons, to enable her to
recover from the desolation and ruin which the baleful
policy of Louis and his Catholic advisers had wrought.

The injury to France in the matter of population
is reckoned by different writers at from 300,000 to
500,000; but both in this respect, and as regards
the distribution of the exiles throughout the different
countries which afforded them shelter, reliable statistics are difficult to obtain. Taking the registers of
the French churches in England, where the refugees
naturally reported themselves on arrival, Weiss esti-
mates that 85,000 landed here in the ten years preceding and following the Revocation. But this number
is as likely to be under as over the mark; for the
same writer admits that the consistories never
furnished complete lists to the English authorities,
for fear of inspiring the jealousy of the inhabitants,
and closing the door to future immigrants. Just as
unreliable are the statistics which bear on the mone-
tary loss to France. Poole, however, gives an excel-
lent illustration of the damage suffered by that
country in this respect. Citing authorities, he observes that the rate of interest on the Amsterdam
Exchange, in 1684, went from $3\frac{1}{2}$ to 3 per cent. and
to 2 per cent. in 1687, owing to the influx of specie
from abroad, whilst at the same time the French
Exchequer had to make up the loss by the universal
use of paper currency.

The effects of the cruel and stupid policy, pursued
through so many successive generations and culmin-
ating in the revocation of the Edict of Nantes, became

in course of time as visible in the moral as in the material condition of France. With a ruined trade and a credit exhausted by war, the population soon became mutinous, and openly defied the authority of the government. The horrors of Saint Bartholomew and the Dragonnades also taught their lesson. Those who had been among the most bigoted persecutors of the Protestants revolted against their own leaders; the principles of the Encyclopædists became the gospel of the people, and the majesty of the Church fell into contempt. Long pent up feelings of resentment against tyranny and privilege at length broke through all barriers of restraint, and the atrocities of the Revocation found their Nemesis in the excesses of the Revolution.

It is generally conceded that the English were originally a purely pastoral and agricultural people, who were dependent upon foreign markets for many articles of clothing and manufacture which could not be produced by their ordinary domestic industries. Large quantities of wool, it is true, were produced here and exported to foreign countries; but the skilled workmen of Germany, France, and Flanders dyed and wove it into cloth for our use as well as their own. An outbreak of war, therefore, occasioned great distress on both sides of the channel. We in that case had

no market for our fleeces, and those who were dependent upon us for their supply were driven to despair,
for want of the raw material with which to keep
their looms going. Smiles says that when hostilities
broke out, and communication between the two shores
was interrupted, as much distress was occasioned in
Flanders as in our own day was experienced in Lancashire by the stoppage of the supply of cotton from
the United States.

The inconvenience of having to send abroad for our
cloth was so much felt, that as early as the reign of
Edward III. large numbers of Flemish weavers came
over, at the invitation of the king, induced by the
high wages and ample employment offered, and settled
in London, Kent, Yorkshire, Lancashire, and other
places. Successive English kings, down to the time of
Henry VIII., pursued a like policy and encouraged the
immigration of skilled artisans of all classes, such as
armourers, cutlers, brewers, miners, and ship-builders,
the principal workmen employed by the Court being
Flemings and Germans.

When Edward VI. came to the throne, it was no
longer necessary to hold out inducements for foreign
workmen, persecuted for their faith, to come and settle
here; the sympathy had been established, and skilled
labour flowed to England of its own accord. Latimer's
wish that valuable persons might be induced to settle
in this country as a means of "insuring its pros-

perity " was realized ; for foreigners were soon to be found in nearly every important town in England " diligently pursuing their several callings." The influx of Flemings, however, at length became so considerable that the native population petitioned the authorities to put a stop to it, and an estimate was ordered to be made of the foreigners in London.

In the reign of Elizabeth persecuted Protestants arrived in still larger numbers, landing naturally on those parts of the coast nearest to France and Flanders, namely, at Dover, Deal, Sandwich, Harwich, and Yarmouth. Maidstone, Canterbury and Norwich also offered them shelter. The Queen immediately gave them her countenance and protection, writing to the Mayor and Commonalty of one of the places named, strongly recommending them as likely greatly to benefit the town by teaching the inhabitants knowledge in " sundry handycrafts " ; and she specially instances the trades the foreigners were to carry on, such as the " makinge of says, bays, and other cloth which hath not been used to be made in this our realme of Englonde." Immediately the refugees landed they began to pursue their various industries under the protection of the local authorities ; from all of which it would seem that England was not in those days the great market of the world for those textile manufactures in which she now excels.

Again we read that, the year after the Flemings

came to Sandwich, and for several years in succession, numbers of French people, of all ages and sexes, fleeing from their country, arrived at Rye, on the Sussex coast, some in open boats, and in mid-winter. The Mayor of Rye, writing to Lord Burleigh in 1572, states that "between the 27th of August and the 4th of November no fewer than 641 had landed." It would appear from the records existing that the refugees were of all sorts and conditions: private gentlemen, doctors, ministers of religion, students, schoolmasters, tradesmen, mariners, mechanics, and labourers. Being more or less destitute, collections were made for them throughout England, the poor Flemings who had previously landed at Sandwich giving from their own slender resources help to the destitute Frenchmen in their need.

As the persecutions increased in severity in France and Flanders, those who fled for safety continued to arrive in still larger numbers,—cloth makers from Antwerp and Bruges, lace makers from Valenciennes, cambric makers from Cambray, and glass makers from Paris, who as they landed were despatched to different parts of England, where they maintained themselves by their different trades. Facilities were also given them for observing their own forms of worship, and as early as the reign of Edward VI. churches were set apart for them in London, Norwich, Southampton, and Canterbury. Throughout their wanderings they

seem to have preserved the settled purpose of worship-
ping God in their own way, and their fasts and thanks-
givings generally had reference to events that had
occurred abroad, or that marked periods of calamity or
deliverance in their history. The records of " God's
House" at Southampton, which was resorted to from
an early date both by French and Flemings, contain
many interesting entries; services, for example, relating to the persecutions by the Duke of Alva, the
defeat of the Prince of Condé at the battle of Jarnac,
the ravages of the plague, the shock of an earthquake,
the appearance of a comet, the defeat of the Spanish
Armada. The last-mentioned event seems to have
filled the hearts of the little congregation with joy, and
they united in public thanksgiving for the wonderful
dispersion of the Spanish Fleet and the protection of
this kingdom from the tyranny of the Pope. A few
days later another fast was held for the purpose of
beseeching a blessing upon the English navy for
putting the Armada to flight. Another interesting
memento of the foreign exiles exists to the present
day in the Walloon or French chapel situate in the
undercroft of Canterbury Cathedral, where, with the
permission of the liberal-minded Archbishop Parker,
the "gentle and profitable strangers," as he termed
them, were permitted to conduct their worship in their
own language, teach their children, and even set up
their looms and carry on their trades.

When the Flemings first settled at Sandwich, the town, which had originally been one of considerable importance, had fallen into decay, and the inhabitants were in great distress. Immediately on their arrival, however, it began to wear a more thriving aspect; looms were started for the manufacture of different kinds of cloth, and bi-weekly markets, which were resorted to by London merchants, were established. Other branches of industry were also promoted; windmills were erected for the first time near the town, and smiths, brewers, hat-makers, carpenters, shipwrights, and potters began busily to labour at their different callings. All these trades the native population learned of the strangers, and general prosperity ensued.

Gardening, which had become a lost art in England, was re-introduced, the vegetables grown by the Flemings being so much in demand in London that many of them removed from Sandwich to the neighbourhood of the metropolis, where they started the market gardens of Battersea, Bermondsey, and Wandsworth. Before they arrived here the people of the Low Countries had been noted for their horticulture; it is even said that Katherine, the Queen of Henry VIII., used to send to Flanders for her salads, not being able to procure one in the whole of England. Whether this be true or not, it is admitted by writers of the time that in the sixteenth century nearly all vegetables were imported from abroad, and were very dear and a great luxury. Smiles, quoting from Hartlib, says that in 1650 an old man then living remembered "the first gardener who came into Surrey to plant cabbages and cauliflowers, and to sow turnips, carrots, parsnips, and early pease, all of which at that time were great wonders, we having few or none in England but what came from Holland or Flanders." The introduction of the hop plant into Kent has also been attributed to the Protestant Walloons.

Many refugees also settled in London, where they carried on their different trades. The Borgeny, or Petty Bergundy, in the district of Bermondsey, took its name from its foreign residents, as did Joiner's Street, in the same vicinity, from the skilled Flemish carpenters who worked there. In Bermondsey the Flemings also started breweries and tanneries and the manufacture of felt hats. The free school of St. Olave's, in Southwark, owes its foundation to the benevolence of one Henry Leck, or Hock, a brewer from Wesel. The famous dye works at Bow were established by Peter de Croix and Dr. Kepler, the white cloth of England having previously been sent abroad to be dyed, and when re-imported sold as Flemish. The making of brass plates for kitchen utensils, of pendulum or Dutch clocks, arras, tapestry, printed paper hangings, articles of jewellery, cutlery, and mathematical instruments was introduced by the

French and Flemish workmen, who settled in Mort-
lake, Fulham, and different parts of London.

A French refugee named Briot, who had been chief
engraver of moneys coined during the reign of Louis
XIII. of France, was the first to introduce the coin-
ing-press into England, and in or about 1633 was
appointed Chief Engraver to the Mint. Foreign
merchants also settled in the city, where they infused
new life and enterprise into commercial undertakings.
Want of space precludes me from mentioning the
names of many leading foreign merchants who in
Queen Elizabeth's time acquired great weight and
influence in London; but their wealth may be judged
from the fact that to a voluntary loan raised by the
Queen they largely subscribed in sums of £100 and
upwards.

Although the jealousy of the native population was
frequently directed against the refugees, they continued to come over in increasing numbers. From a
census taken in 1621 it would appear that 10,000 had
already settled in London alone, where they carried
on 121 different trades and occupations. So as not
to interfere too much with each other, the foreigners
availed themselves of the royal license, and settled in
different parts of the country.

Norwich is a remarkable instance of the beneficial
results arising from the importation of foreign enterprise and methods of manufacture, as well as of the

narrow spirit which from time to time sought to restrict the strangers in the free exercise of the very
industries they had originally taught the inhabitants.

Although the commercial importance of this city
was mainly owing to the energy and example of the
Protestant settlers, the local guilds passed such stringent rules against foreign labour, that the Flemings at
last left Norwich and went to Leeds, Wakefield, and
other places where they were allowed to prosecute
their trades without molestation. When they had
gone the industries of Norwich gradually fell into
decay, the population diminished, houses stood un-
occupied, riots occurred among the workpeople, and
it was even proposed in Parliament to raze the place
to the ground. To put an end to so disastrous a
state of things the Mayor and Corporation, accompanied by the principal citizens, went in deputation
to the Duke of Norfolk, urging him to use his influence to procure a fresh settlement of foreign artisans,
in the place of those who had left. The Duke succeeded in inducing 300 families, Dutch and Walloon,
who were followed by others, to establish themselves
at his charge, upon which the manufacture of says,
bays, serges, arras, mouchade, bombazines, flowered
silks, damasks, and other articles of foreign importation
was begun. The cultivation of garden produce was
introduced, employment was found for the people,
food became cheap, trade remunerative, and the city

shortly regained its former prosperity, Bishop Park-
hurst stating as his conviction " that these blessings
from God have happened by reason of the godly
exiles who were here so kindly harboured." Later
on the townsfolk again became jealous of foreigners,
but Queen Elizabeth and the local authorities inter-
fered, and the settlers were allowed to pursue their
occupations in peace.

As regards the material wealth—apart from industrial knowledge and enterprise—which the French
and Flemish refugees brought into this country, it is
difficult to form a correct estimate ; but if we take into
consideration the fact that Phillip of Spain derived for
several years many millions of dollars annually from
property left behind by the Protestants of the Low
Countries, and that both there and in France many of
the merchants and others delayed their departure until
they were able, in a measure, to realize their fortunes,
it is not unreasonable to assume that their aggregate
wealth was considerable, although some were so poor
that they brought with them " no other goods but
their children."

Throughout England the industrious strangers from
France and Flanders communicated their skill and
knowledge to the native inhabitants, and everywhere
new branches of trade were started. In the west Flemish weavers set up their looms at Worcester, Evesham,
Droitwich, Kidderminster, Stroud, and Glastonbury.

In the east they also established themselves at Col-
chester, Hertford and Stamford, and at Manchester,
Bolton, Halifax and Kendal in the north. Thus additional sources of employment and fresh branches of industry were opened up to the people of this country, who,
instead of being dependent upon foreign countries for
their supply of cloth and the finer articles of manufacture, began in their turn to make and export them.
In this way we learned the art of thread and lace-
making, thread spun from flax being still known at
Maidstone as "Dutch Work." Lace-makers from
Alençon and Valenciennes settled at Buckingham,
Stoney-Stratford, and Newport-Pagnel, and in the
counties of Bedford, Oxford, Northampton, and Cam-
bridge. The trade in bone lace at Honiton and other
parts of Devonshire was first initiated by exiles
from Antwerp. Foreign immigrants set on foot other
industries also, in which they were more adept than
ourselves, such as working in metals, salt-making and
fish-curing. Newcastle-on-Tyne became noted for
swords, edge-tools and steel implements, the manufacture of which had been introduced by the exiles
from Liège. Sheffield, now so famous for its steel
and iron industries, owes its reputation to the
exquisite skill of Flemish workmen. Yarmouth
and many other places are also indebted for their
knowledge of fishing and herring-curing to the sailors
of the Low Countries who fled to England, the fish

sold in English markets having been previously
caught and cured by the Dutch. The refugees made
their way, moreover, into Ireland and Scotland, where
they introduced such industries as the conditions of
those countries permitted. In 1600 we find a number of Flemings settled in the Canongate of Edinburgh, "making, dressing, and litting of stuffs, giving
great licht and knowledge of their calling to the
country people."

Although a large number of Huguenot fugitives,
after the Revocation, sought asylum in Germany,
Switzerland and Holland, it is estimated that at least
120,000 manufacturers and workmen, principally from
Normandy and the northern towns of France and
Brittany, took refuge here, and introduced the trades
they had practised at home. They were manufacturers of fine linen from Nantes, Rennes, and Morlaix;
clothworkers from Amiens, Abbeville, and Doullens;
gauze and lace-makers from Lille and Valenciennes,
and workmen belonging to various crafts from
towns and cities in the interior. Some of the refugees
were persons of rank, others were physicians, lawyers,
and ministers of religion, but the larger proportion
were artisans and workmen. A Relief Committee was
appointed, and the new-comers were distributed and
provided for according to their capabilities. Some
were placed in commercial houses, others in the army,
others again, for whom employment could not be found

here, were despatched to America; but most of them, being artisans, were provided with tools and employed in English manufactories. They also formed benefit societies for the help of their poorer countrymen, and started workshops of their own, where those who were able to earn a living helped such of their fellows as were unemployed or incapacitated. Smiles remarks that their mutual aid societies were probably, although unacknowledged, the examples from which the Lodges and Benefit Societies of our own labouring classes have since sprung. Whole colonies were founded by the Huguenot refugees in London, where they set up their schools, workshops, factories, and churches. Several districts in the metropolis were almost entirely occupied by them, as, for instance, Spitalfields, Bethnal Green, and Soho. Others distributed themselves in the neighbourhood of the Guildhall, Temple Bar, Long Acre, and the Strand, where they began the manufacture of goods they excelled in making, such as cutlery, surgical and mathematical instruments, watches, clocks, and articles of jewellery and vertu. Well-to-do people in London had previously sent to Paris for things requiring taste and delicate workmanship. We had before that period also imported from France, velvets, satins, silks, gloves, laces, buttons, serges, paper of all sorts, beaver and felt hats, ironmongery, cutlery, linen, salt, soap, pins, needles, combs, and a variety of commodities for household use, some of which are

in our day again imported from that country ; but when
the French artisans settled here, they induced money
" to flow into England instead of out of it ; " articles
previously imported we began to make for ourselves
and export abroad, and in many respects the advantage we then derived has remained with us to this day.

Of all the new industries and sources of wealth introduced into this country by the Huguenot refugees,
none is more worthy of note than the silk trade established by the workmen from Lyons and Tours, first of
all at Canterbury and Blackfriars, and afterwards at
Spitalfields. The latter place finally became the head-
quarters of the silk industry, and from thence it was
extended to other parts of England. The Huguenots
devoted themselves to this trade in all its branches,
introducing new or improving old methods in the
manufacture of brocades, satins, velvets and silks
of all kinds of texture and quality, by which means
we became endowed with a knowledge and skill that
we had formerly envied in our neighbours, and tried
in vain to imitate. Both Elizabeth and James I. had
endeavoured to foster in this country an industry which
had contributed so largely to the prosperity of France,
but it was not until the workmen of Tours and Lyons
had transferred their valuable talents to Spitalfields that
t really took root and became an important branch of
English trade. It is worth mentioning, as showing the
progress we made in this particular business, that

D

according to Keysler, who travelled through Europe in 1730, merchants wishing to sell their silk hose in the kingdom of Naples invariably protested that they were "right English." Not only did we now make silk goods for ourselves, and export to places hitherto supplied by France, but in a comparatively short time our woollen trade enormously increased with those countries from which we had to import raw silk for our looms.

Canterbury and Ipswich also profited considerably by the transfer to our shores of the artistic productions of the French Protestants, and the linen and lace industries which had been introduced by previous refugees were greatly improved. Other useful articles of manufacture, too numerous to describe, were also developed or improved by them. The paper made in England before the Revocation was a common yellow or brown kind, all the finer sorts being imported from France. When the refugees came here they started paper-mills in London, Maidstone, Laverstoke, and other parts of England, and we were soon able to turn out as good paper—even that required for bank notes—as could be bought elsewhere. In the manufacture of glass we had also made little progress, but the glass-makers from Paris, who settled in the Strand, quickly established a reputation, which this country has never lost, for some of the most beautiful productions in glass and crystal.

The Huguenots likewise founded colonies in Scotland. In Edinburgh, where they began the manufacture of linen, a district near Leith Walk is still
called after them ; and Glasgow owes the first paper-
mill ever erected there to a Huguenot who escaped
from France with his little daughter, and managed in
the first days of his exile to earn a bare subsistence
by picking up rags in the street.

Ireland, too, is indebted to the French Protestants
for some of the most important industries which now
flourish in that country. They settled in Dublin,
Waterford, Cork, Kilkenny, Lisburne, and Portarling-
ton, where they introduced their different crafts and
industries. The Irish are noted for their beautiful
linen goods; but few people are aware that it was to
the Huguenots they were indebted for the cultivation of
flax, in all its stages, and the methods originally employed in its manufacture, or that the mixed material
known as "Irish poplin" was originally the endow-
ment of foreign immigrants. It is principally in the
north of Ireland, however, that the Huguenots have left
the most durable record. There the busy industries of
Belfast testify to the generous return made by the
talented and enterprising refugees to whoever received
them with hospitality, and were willing to profit by
their teaching.

If we are tempted to assume with insular self-com-
placency that the rapid growth of our industries, after

the arrival of the foreign fugitives, was chiefly attributable to our own receptive qualities and inherent aptitude, we have but to turn to the pages of Weiss to learn that in whatever other countries the Huguenots settled, the same beneficial results are to be traced. In Brandenburg, the cradle of modern Prussia, in Switzerland, Holland, Denmark, and America—even in Russia and the Cape of Good Hope—wherever the exiles were driven to seek refuge, they communicated to the people who welcomed them their native skill and enterprise, and in each case there ensued a marked improvement in the material condition of the countries of their adoption.

It must not be supposed, however, that the influence of the Huguenots was confined to our industries alone ; nearly every walk and profession in life was enriched by the high and steadfast qualities of our foreign guests. In the annals of literature and science they have left an enduring record ; and many and distinguished are the names of foreign refugees and their decendants, which are to be found on the registers of the Royal Society and the muster-rolls of our Universities. On our own Protestant institutions, too, the strenuous exertions of the French reformers at home in their struggles against Catholicism were not without effect ; neither was the example set by their numerous churches in this country, before the Huguenots became finally absorbed within the Anglican community in creed as well as in language and nationality.

Of the many important services rendered by the Huguenots to this country, not the least notable was the part they played under William, Prince of Orange, in the English rebellion of 1688. When that Prince's intended expedition was made known, large numbers of Huguenots flocked to his standard, and he was able to raise three regiments of infantry and a squadron of cavalry almost entirely from veteran troops who had fought under Schomberg, Turenne, and Condé. Seven hundred Protestant gentlemen of French birth also served as officers in his other regiments. Schomberg himself, an ex-marshal of France, commanded the expedition under the Prince, with secret powers in case his leader should fall; and it was to his politic advice and vast experience that the success of the enterprise, which rid this country of its unconstitutional monarch, was largely due. In his subsequent campaigns in Ireland and elsewhere, William the Third's refugee soldiers and sailors bore themselves with the valour of their chivalrous race, and on many a hard fought field added not only to the laurels of Coutras and Ivry, but also to the fame of British arms.

From the earliest times this country has been subject to a variety of incursions, of which some have left ineffaceable traces on the character and temperament of its inhabitants, whilst others, as in the cases of the

Danish and Roman occupations, are so completely
forgotten that it would almost require the microscopic
eye of the archæologist to discover any evidences
remaining. But neither the Saxon settlement, which
contributed so materially to the constituent elements
of our race and language, nor the Norman conquest,
to which we are indebted for our inclusion within the
circle of civilized nations, was pregnant with mor
momentous consequences to this country, from the
point of view of material prosperity, than the advent
of the busy, quick-witted and cultivated strangers
who enriched us with their rare skill and novel industries. Any excess of description in dealing with so
interesting a theme is to be condemned; it would
detract from the merits of the picture and injure the
impression it is sought to convey. But when we com
pare the commanding position our country now enjoys
as an essentially industrial and trading power, with
that which it occupied in this respect when France
and Spain drove from their midst the flower of their
population, it is surely no exaggeration to say that
the friendly invasion of the Huguenots and Flemings
may be regarded as one of the most eventful incidents
in our national history.

SHOULD GOVERNMENT INTERFERE?

By Montague Crackanthorpe.

The Preliminary Report of the recent census has been awaited with impatience by all who take an interest in the Social Problems of the day. What we have been anxious to learn with certainty is—(1) the mode in which our population is distributed throughout the country; (2) its rate of annual increase calculated on the average of the last ten years. The returns have now been sufficiently analysed to furnish this information, and to enable us to deduce several conclusions of very great importance.

The population of England and Wales, which at the end of the reign of Elizabeth was under five millions, is now twenty-nine millions. Its rate of increase—meaning by this the excess of births over deaths—calculated on the average of the last ten years, is about 300,000 per annum. Mr. Mundella stated a short time ago that we were "growing a Birmingham a year." As the population of Birmingham is nearly 400,000, it would have been more correct to say that we grow three Birminghams in four years. It is true that, owing to causes which will be indicated presently, the actual population falls short of the estimate made by the Registrar-General by 800,000, the rate of increase having diminished of late. Thus in 1871-81 it was 14·36 per cent., whereas in 1881-91 it was 11·65. Again, in 1890, the natural increase of the population by excess of births over deaths was 303,267, while the average increase in the five preceding years was 366,013. This is so far satisfactory. But as the numbers accumulate on the principle on which money accumulates when invested at compound interest, the rapidity of growth is enormous.

If, indeed, the twenty-nine millions were all provided with food, clothes, and lodging, there would be no cause for uneasiness. But, unfortunately, this is far from being the case. A large proportion is composed of those who are either unable to support themselves or have no desire to do so. Here are a few facts. In 1890, no less than 611,000 of the inhabitants of England and Wales were in receipt of poor law relief, 179,000 being assisted in the workhouse and 462,000 out of it. Taking the average of the first quarter of the present year, the number of these paupers had increased to 700,526, of whom 186,337 were receiving indoor and 514,189 outdoor relief. This amounts to 23·5 per 1,000 of the population. Again, take another test, as supplied by the Register of Deaths. In the last quarter of 1890, out of the total deaths registered in England and Wales, 11 in every 100 occurred in workhouses, hospitals, and public lunatic asylums. After making allowance for the fact that many

persons not belonging to the pauper class may be
found in public hospitals, we may safely infer that
one in every ten of the above 11 per cent. was dependent either on the bounty of the State or on that of
private individuals.

When we come to consider the condition of the
Metropolis, the figures are still more instructive.
First, take Inner London—that is to say, the London
which embraces the area of the administrative county
of London, and also the "City" or municipal London. This Inner London, we may remark in passing,
is the same as the London of the Registrar-General
(otherwise termed Registration London), provided the
small hamlet of Penge, which lies outside "Registration London" but inside the "county of London,"
is excepted from it. Now, the population of this
Inner London, which covers 77,110 acres, was, as
enumerated last April, 4,211,056. In 1881 it was
3,816,483, showing an increase in ten years of 394,573,
or about 10 per cent. All round Inner London lies
what is conveniently called the Outer Ring, comprising Enfield, Staines, Uxbridge, Edgware, Harrow,
Watford, Hendon, Chipping Barnet, Totteridge, Ches-
hunt, East Ham, Walthamstow, Erith, Farnborough,
the Grays, Chiselhurst, Carshalton, Epsom, Kingston-
on-Thames, Richmond, Hampton, Hanwell. This vast
area covers 370,924 acres, and contained, in 1881, a
population of 950,173. That population had grown

last April to 1,422,276, an increase in the ten years of
472,098. The Inner and the Outer Rings, which
taken together constitute "Greater London," showed
on the last census night a population of 5,633,332. In
1881 this population was 4,766,661; so that, compar-
ing one census with another, the total increase of
"Greater London" in the last ten years has been
866,671, or at the rate of over 18 per cent.

The growth of the districts immediately contiguous
to the Metropolis has been truly surprising. It
will be sufficient to give a few instances. The population of Plaistow and Tottenham has considerably
more than doubled since 1881. In Tottenham the
actual rise has been from 46,000 to 97,000. Hornsey
has increased by 24,000 during the same period,
Willesden by nearly 34,000, Croydon by 27,000. A
like expansion has been going on at the same time in
our large provincial towns. Cardiff has grown by 56
per cent., Newcastle by 28 per cent., Portsmouth by
24, Leeds by nearly 19, Birkenhead and Oldham by
rather more than 18. In fact, town growth has been
the almost universal rule. The one remarkable exception has been Liverpool, the population of which has
decreased. This is probably to be explained by the
fact that the area of official enumeration does not
coincide with that of the extended district.

Now let us look at the statistics of the pauperism of
London corresponding to those already given for the

whole of England and Wales. Inside the Metropolitan area 5,000 able-bodied men are "relieved" every day, at a cost to the Metropolitan ratepayers of £188,000 a year. This is the testimony of the living. Let us now listen to that of the dead. In 1890 the number of deaths recorded in "Registration London" was 91,243. Of these 31 were caused by sheer starvation, and of the rest 21,881, or 24 per cent., occurred in institutions supported by the rates or by voluntary contributions. This 24 per cent was made up thus : 12·3 per cent., or 1 in every 8, died in workhouses ; 8·5 per cent., or 1 in every 12, died in general hospitals ; 2·1 per cent, or 1 in every 48, died in lunatic and imbecile asylums ; and the remaining 1·1 per cent., or 1 in every 90, died in the hospitals for infectious diseases under control of the Metropolitan Asylums Board. The last returns to hand as we write are as follows. In the first week of August, 1891, the number of Metropolitan paupers (exclusive of vagrants and lunatics in asylums) was—indoor, 53,827; outdoor, 30,851 ; total, 84,678. A record of poverty this, for the hot season of the year, that may well set all Londoners a-thinking !

When a vital organ of the body is overcharged and its active functions are suspended in consequence, doctors are in the habit of saying that the patient is suffering from congestion of that organ. A similar malady prevails in England at the present moment.

London is the heart of England, and the above figures show that London is congested. If it were not, there would be no overcrowding such as we see in the poorer districts of the Metropolis, and there would be no sweating such as disgraces its Eastern quarter. How does a physician in the case of the human body seek to relieve the congested part? First, by studying the causes of the flow to it, and next by endeavouring to arrest this flow by every means in his power. The Social Reformer proceeds on the same lines in dealing with the population problem. Having ascertained the yearly rate of increase, he proceeds to ask himself two questions: (1) To what is this rate of increase due? (2) Can any means be suggested, consistently with religion and sound morality, for keeping it within moderate bounds?

The answers to these questions are not far to seek. Assuming the death and emigration rates to remain the same, increase of population is obviously due either to growth from within or to influx from without. Now, growth from within, or, in other words, the number of fresh births, varies very considerably in different grades of society. It is a curious but established fact that the half-starved and the destitute multiply far more rapidly than the well-nourished and the well-to-do. So frequently has this been noticed, that able writers—for instance, Mr. Thomas Doubleday, in his "True Law of Population" (1841)—have ascribed the phenomenon to physiological causes. Mr. Herbert Spencer, in his " Principles of Biology " (vol. ii. part 6), maintains, however, that this is an error, and in contradiction to the course of nature as observed in the animal kingdom. We do not care to enter into this controversy now. Assuming Mr. Spencer to be right and Mr. Doubleday wrong, the relative infertility of the comfortable classes is only the more significant. It points to the exercise of prudence and forethought on their part. It shows also that everything that tends to raise the standard of living tends also to diminish abnormal rapidity of growth. It shows, further, that everything which, like the sweating system, tends to keep down wages, and therefore to lower the standard of living, must tend in the opposite direction. The practical importance of this last conclusion will appear later on.

Before leaving this point there is one other observation to be made. The State cannot, it is true, control the number of births, but it can directly encourage their increase. At present it does this in a mischievous way. In England we have an absurd law by which boys of the age of twelve and girls of the age of fourteen are permitted to contract a valid marriage. That this license is largely availed of, the marriages at our East End churches show. In France the marriageable age is eighteen in the case of males and fifteen in the case of females. Again, in England the consent of the parents of minors is not necessary to validate a marriage. In France, no male under twenty-five and no female under twenty-one can marry without the consent of both parents, or of the survivor of them if only one be living. It is an obvious, and would be a salutary, reform to raise the age of marriage in England to sixteen in the case of girls, and to eighteen in the case of young men. Education and a just sense of parental responsibility must be trusted to do the rest. The labourer, both in town and country, must learn that he has no right to bring children into the world whom he has no prospect of maintaining. This, as we have said, is the maxim of the upper and middle classes, as well as of the best of our artisans. In fact, its general acceptance amongst these is the true cause of the decline of the birth rate during the last ten years to which we adverted at the opening of this paper. The teaching which has long influenced the higher social strata has now to be extended to the strata below, until at length it permeates the entire community.

The second cause of increase—influx from without —is of a twofold kind. It is caused either by migration from the provinces to London and other large towns, or by immigration from abroad. The rush to the towns from the country is due, in part, to the fact that hand-labour has been largely superseded by machinery; in part, to the fact that the agricultural

labourer has, owing to enclosures and the consolidation
of small holdings, become divorced from the soil; in
part, also, to the improvements in locomotion, to the
attraction of the higher wages of the town, and to the
love of change and excitement which is innate in the
human breast. We cannot put back the clock of time,
or divert a stream of tendency by any legislative
enactment, but we can enhance the attractiveness of
our rural districts by facilitating the acquisition of
land by the labourer, so as to relieve the monotony of
his toil. The Allotment Acts, of which the earliest
dates as far back as 1815, and the latest is in 1890,
were passed with this view. The later Acts have been
attended with most satisfactory results; the number of
allotments having been 246,000 in 1873; in 1886,
357,000; and in 1890, 454,000. The Small Holdings
Bill of Mr. Jesse Collings is a further step in the
same direction, doing on a small scale for the English
peasant what the Ashbourne Act has already done for
the Irish. The stimulus given to technical instruction
in agriculture, by the appropriations to that purpose
recently voted by County Councils out of their share
of the £743,000 transferred from the Imperial exchequer under the Act of 1890, will greatly aid the
new occupying owners to make the most of their land
when they get it. These measures have been sorely
wanted, as will appear from the following fact. The
total number of males and females engaged in agri-

cultural work and food production at the present day
is one and a half millions, being barely one-half of the
number so engaged a century ago. In 1769, Arthur
Young estimated that out of a total population of
8,500,000 the agricultural class numbered 2,800,000,
a proportion of one in every three. With our existing
population of 29 millions, the proportion is only one in
every nineteen.

In considering the increase of population due to
immigration from abroad, we propose to leave open
the question whether the influx of pauper foreigners
has, or has not, been of such magnitude during the
last ten years as to displace large bodies of British
workmen or materially reduce wages. At present, one
set of persons appears to be engaged in minimising,
another set in maximising, the figures. It is by no
means an easy task to strike the balance between them.
It will be sufficient for the present purpose to refer to
the report of the Secretary of the Commercial Department of the Board of Trade, issued last March. "I
see no reason to doubt," says Mr. Giffen, a thoroughly
impartial witness, and one whom the minimisers constantly quote, "that there has been a substantial increase in the immigration of aliens into London in
1890, and an increase of that special immigration
which has attracted so much attention of late years—
that of Polish Jews, many of whom are in a state of
great poverty, and some of actual destitution." It is

beyond dispute that the arrivals in London in 1890 of aliens of every description were about 4,000 more than in 1889, the total number of the former arrivals being placed at about 9,000 by the Chief Commissioner of Police of the Metropolis. But 1890 is hardly a safe criterion by which to gauge 1891, owing to the recent action of the Czar and of the Government of the United States. The imperial ukase issued a few months ago for the expulsion of the Jews from Russia has, according to authentic accounts, brought about a veritable exodus to the South. They were reported recently as leaving Moscow at the rate of 100 to 150 a week. Thousands were then preparing to quit Kieff; and the arrivals of these unhappy refugees at the port of Hamburg and on the frontiers of Austria were becoming more frequent day by day.

Now, what is the destination of all these exiles, many of whom are wholly without money and ignorant of any trade? They can no longer make their way to New York, for the law of March last excludes from the United States "all paupers or persons who are likely to become a public charge." They are equally excluded by statute law from Canada and most of our Australian colonies—*e.g.*, Victoria, South Australia, Tasmania, and New Zealand; the only colonies in which there are no prohibitive immigration statutes being New South Wales, Queensland, Western Australia, Cape Colony, and Natal. These, we may be

E

sure, will quickly follow the example set them by the rest, and if England alone remains passive, she may soon find herself exposed to an invasion from the East of Europe of an alarming, albeit peaceful, character.

What is her duty in these circumstances, and what are her rights ?

It can hardly be disputed that every civilized State is entitled to make what regulations it pleases both as to emigration from, and immigration into, its territory. Every such State may, for instance, on the breaking out of hostilities with another State, refuse to allow any resident in it, whether permanent or temporary, to depart beyond its boundaries if his services are desired for home defence. It may also refuse to allow any person to cross its frontier or land upon its shores whom it regards as likely to be dangerous to its internal peace. Witness the Alien Expulsion Acts passed by us in 1793, 1815, and 1848. On the same principle it may decline, as the United States Government has declined, to admit any one who is likely to become a public or private charge by reason of any defect, physical or mental, disabling him from performing the duties of citizenship. Thus much will be conceded as a matter of international law. [1]

---

[1] See the recent case, before the Privy Council, of *Musgrove* v. *Chun Teeong Toy* (1891) App. Cas. 272, and authorities there cited.

Let us now push the argument a little further, with the help of one or two illustrations from life.

An Italian padrone arrives in England with some forty or fifty children. These children he has hired, or rather bought, from their parents in the picturesque but squalid villages of Calabria at a very low figure. They are brought by him over here to earn money in the streets of our towns, in order that their master may end his days in his native land as a country gentleman of independent means. All of us have seen such children in different parts of London, though, unless we have lived in the neighbourhood of Hatton Garden, we shall probably know nothing of their *entrepreneur.* That this business exists and flourishes was affirmed not long ago by Signor Righetti, the Secretary of the Italian Benevolent Society. As the nationality of the imported foreigner is only an accident, take another illustration from the far East of Europe. A party of Syrian Arabs was despatched from Marseilles (by whom it is not known, nor is it at all material), with their passages paid to New York. They had with them no money to speak of, and they had no prospects of earning any. They were carried through to Havre, and thence to Liverpool, but when they reached New York they were refused permission to land by the American authorities. The American vessel which took them out had to bring them back to Havre, where they were kept at the public expense

for about six weeks. At the end of that time the
Havre people coaxed a captain of a British vessel
to bring them again to Liverpool, the Liverpool
authorities having, as the law now stands, no right to
reject them. In Liverpool they remained for several
months as pauper inmates of the workhouse there,
until at last a subscription was got up to send them to
their own country. This case was vouched for by the
vestry clerk of Liverpool in his evidence before the
Committee of the House of Commons on Foreign
Immigration in May, 1889. Will any one deny that
it would have been better, not only for the Lancashire
ratepayers, but for these Oriental paupers themselves,
if the British authorities had been armed with power
to refuse them access here in the first instance, and to
compel the skipper of the ship that brought them to
take them away to their place of embarkation at his
own cost and charges?

Now, let us take the other class of case referred
to a few pages back, and which occurs on the average
twice a week in the East End of our metropolis. A
number of Russian and Polish Jews—the religion is
not of the essence, any more than the nationality—
reach the port of London from Hamburg. Their property consists of a bit of dry bread and a piece of
mouldy cheese, with possibly a herring or two tied
up in a cotton handkerchief. The purpose of their
coming is to compete for employment in the English

labour market. Their standard of living being ex-
cessively low, they are able to do this with advantage.
Many of them are agricultural labourers; others have
some little skill in tailoring, in making boots, shoes,
and slippers, and in a kind of light carpentering,
which turns out cheap furniture and knick-knacks.
The foul air of the sweater's den does not tell on their
constitutions, already enured to greater hardships in
the overstocked and plague-stricken towns and
villages in South Russia from which they have just
emerged. Ought the British Government to decline to
receive them? This question is a more complex one
than the preceding, and to answer it satisfactorily
we must look into the case a little more closely.

And, first, let us remark that any one who desires
to satisfy himself of the characteristics of these
" greeners " should pay a visit some Sunday morning
to Goulston Street, Whitechapel. He will there find
specimens of them standing at the street corner, on
the look-out for some one to hire them. The ear may
recognise them at once by their use of the Jüdisch
language, and the eye by their top boots, which probably have never left their feet during the whole of
the journey to London. If we inquire what are their
antecedents, and why they have come so far on so
unpromising an errand, we shall probably find it is
not by their own fault. Since the days of Catherine
II. the Russian laws have been very severe on the

Jews. Some six millions of them remain caged up within the pale of settlement in Southern Russia, the boundaries of which are prescribed by imperial edict. In most parts of the pale they are reported, by those who have made it their business to ascertain the facts, to be treated, not as men, but as lower animals, or even insects. In Berditscheff, in the government of Kieff, the official statistics state, apparently without a twinge of conscience, that they are huddled together more like salted herrings than human beings. Tens of thousands of them are devoid of any constant means of subsistence, living from hand to mouth. Several families are often crowded into one or two rooms of a dilapidated hut, so that at night there is absolutely no space whatever between the sleepers. The lodgers turn their rooms into workshops in the daytime, refining wax therein, making tallow candles, tanning leather, and doing other like unsavoury things. Whole families live, work, sleep, and eat together in that fetid atmosphere, with their tools and materials lying around on all sides.

Again, the *Moscow Gazette*, speaking of the same town, says :—

"The streets of the Jewish quarter are not more than four feet wide. On either side of them the tumble-down old houses seem ready to fall to pieces. Children are lying before the houses in the street in a state of almost complete nudity, wallowing in the slough, the mothers of these children sleeping in the midst of them, stretched out sideways and longways under the rays of the burning sun." [1]

We do not, of course, mean to affirm that all, or any, of the Russian Jews who arrive here in search of work come from this town of Berditscheff. It does not matter to the argument whether they do or not, provided we assume, as it is conceived we may, that Berditscheff furnishes a fair average specimen of the native condition of the class to which these immigrants belong. Neither is it alleged that every such immigrant arrives here without a farthing in his pocket. But at the best their store is a scanty one, and, in spite of police precautions, it often falls into the hands of unscrupulous crimps, who are in the pay of the low lodging-house keeper, or of the master sweater.

An accurate description of the mode in which these miserable folk live in London was given by Mr. Lakeman, one of our Factory Inspectors, in his evidence before the Sweating Commission.

" The habits of these people are very, very dirty ; they seem almost to revel in dirt, rather than in cleanliness. Going into some workshops, you find a filthy bed, on which garments which are made are laid, children perfectly naked lying about the floor and on the beds ; frying-pans and all sorts of dirty utensils, with food of various descriptions, on the

---

[1] See the interesting article on the Jews in Russia, signed " E. B. Lanin," in the *Fortnightly Review*, October, 1890.

bed, under the bed, over the bed—everywhere; clothes hanging on a line, with a large gas stove to dry them, the ashes all falling about, and the atmosphere so dense that you get ill after a night's work there. The temperature as tested by me was found to be 90 ."

The economical effect of the introduction of large batches of men who can exist under such conditions as these is obvious: (1) They drive out of employment a corresponding number of Englishmen. (2) They lower the standard of living all round, and by this means reduce the wage-rate, which is determined by the local standard of living, and not by an imaginary wages fund. (3) They give direct encouragement to the system of sweating, by which unscrupulous sub-contractors contrive to grind the faces of the poor. (4) They breed great discontent in the localities where the foreign immigrants are found, tending to foster international and even inter-religious hatred. Here is the experience of Mr. Freak, the Secretary of the Shoemakers' Society, when questioned by the Immigration Committee.

" I know that at the time when I first came to London any one could get work at the middle or common class of goods, and now the price is reduced so low that to work single-handed a man cannot get a living. He has to sweat his children and his wife, and if a man and his wife and children do not want anything more than just bread and cheese and sleep, then they may get a living out of it, because some of these Jews that come over will not come out of the house for a whole week; they will sleep in the same place where they

work day after day, and they simply get food and the barest
raiment to cover them, and that is all they get for their
work."

As long as we permit the East End of London and
our other large centres of industry to be invaded
with impunity by people of this class, it is waste of
energy to attempt to restrict our numbers in the
towns, either by raising the age of marriage, or by
schemes for settling the agricultural labourer on the
land. Our efforts in the cause of emigration, are, for
the same reason, both senseless and abortive. What
is the use of empowering Guardians of the Poor and
County Councils to raise money on the rates for trans-
planting our native paupers elsewhere, if for every
destitute Englishman we send out of the country we
let a destitute foreigner in ? Of what avail are our
thirty-seven Emigration Societies—there are, at least,
six of them in London alone—if their work of deple-
tion is to be undone at one end as soon as it is begun
at the other. One might as well try to empty a reser-
voir by opening a waste pipe at the bottom of it without shutting off the pipe of inflow at the top. It is
the old fable of the Danaids' sieve, with blood passing
through it instead of water.

But we are told by the sentimentalists that con-
sistency is, after all, a poor business, and that to
pass any restrictive measure would be a grave
breach of hospitality, and an infraction of the

moral law. This argument involves a slight con-
fusion of thought. A political asylum is one thing;
a refuge for the destitute is another. It is not proposed in any way to interfere with the immunity
which England has long secured to those who fly to
it to escape persecution in their own country on
account of their political or religious convictions, and
who are not charged with any ordinary crime known
to the English Courts. But a State is not bound to
admit the foreign pauper who can only thrive at the
cost of the independence of its own citizens, any more
than it is bound to give shelter and sanctuary to the
foreign fugitive from justice. Just as the surrender
of the one is a duty prescribed by international law,
the breach of which would be a violation of the moral
obligations binding on civilized countries, so the
exclusion of the other is a duty which the nation
owes to itself, the breach of which would be an act
of national suicide. Besides, it is an entire mistake
to suppose that this right of asylum for political
offences is peculiar to England, and that in this respect we have a character to keep up which places us
on a pinnacle among the nations. It is now exactly
half a century since a French Minister of Justice
issued a famous State paper, in which, after correctly
stating the principles on which the practice of extradition rests, he laid it down that offences of a
political character formed an important exception to
the general rule :—

"Les crimes politiques s'accomplissent dans des circon-
stances si difficiles à apprécier, ils naissent de passions si
ardentes, qui souvent sont leur excuse, que La France main-
tient le principe que l'extradition *ne doit pas avoir lieu pour
fait politique*. C'est une règle qu'elle met son honneur à
soutenir. Elle a toujours refusé, depuis 1830, de pareilles
extraditions; elle n'en demandera jamais."

  *   *   *   *   *

Another argument sometimes urged against excluding the pauper foreigner is that to do so would
be rank Protection, and directly contrary to the
principles of Free Trade. The answer to this may be
given in a sentence. Living human bodies are not
commodities, and in the presence of the sweaters' dens
free competition is a delusion and a snare. The Polish
Jew drives the British workman out of the labour
market just as a base currency drives a pure currency
out of circulation. The British workman is as capable
as the foreigner of manufacturing slop clothing, but
he cannot compete successfully with the latter unless
he is willing to work for merely nominal wages and
under insanitary conditions revolting even to read
of. Nor is it merely a question of numbers. As Mr.
Hobson well puts it in his "Problems of Poverty"
(Methuen & Co., 1891): "Where work is slack and
difficult to get, a very small addition of low living
foreigners will cause a perceptible fall in the entire
wages of the neighbourhood in the employment which
their competition affects." It is true that the Jew

does not long continue working on starvation wages,
and that he often rises by his industry and skill to
the position of a master sweater or the dignity of a
petty tradesman. But this is of no avail so long as
when one intruder quits the ranks another forthwith
enlists. Herein lies the gist of the nuisance. It is
not the mere fact of foreign immigration that damages
us. It is its persistent and increasing flow.

But, it may be asked, Is it not the fact that
England has in modern times greatly benefited by
the introduction of foreign labour? Undoubtedly it
is, as, for instance, when the Flemings came over
here in the reign of Edward III., and again in still
greater numbers after the sacking of Antwerp in 1585.
The same is true of the Huguenots who were driven
to our shores exactly a century later by the revocation
of the Edict of Nantes (1685). But the circumstances
were wholly different. The Flemings, by introducing
a finer kind of weaving, and the Huguenots, by estab-
lishing new branches of the silk, glass, and paper
manufacture, conferred a direct and positive benefit
upon English commerce. Both alike brought with
them considerable capital, and neither entered into
ruinous competition with our own working classes.
There is as much resemblance between these immigrants and the Polish Jew as there is between the art
of painting and the manufacture of garments from
shoddy cloth.

If precedents for State interference are asked for, we may refer to what took place some years ago on the western seaboard of the United States, when the Chinese were swarming into California. It was then urged on behalf of the new immigrants that they had created a trade in the country which they had adopted as their home. For example, that they made cigars, and that no cigars had been made in California before. That they also made shoes and built railroads, and reclaimed swamp lands, none of which things had the native settler cared to do so long as the population had remained scattered and scanty. The answer of the United States Commissioners was complete. Circumstances had altered since then. "The Chinaman had begun to displace the white man. If Chinese immigration concentrated in cities where it threatened public order, or *if it confined itself to localities where it was an injury to the interests of the American people,* the Government of the United States had no hesitation in taking steps to prevent its continuance." If we alter "American" to "English," the contingency which we have placed in italics has already been realized in Whitechapel and several of our northern towns.

* * * * *

One or two practical suggestions, in conclusion, as to what ought to be done. The first and obvious step is to collect more precise information than we at

present possess as regards the nationalities of these
pauper immigrants, where they have last come from,
and whither they are bound. The machinery for
this is ready to our hand. In 1836 was passed
the last of the series of Acts known as the Alien
Acts, the history of which is given in detail in
another part of this volume. This Act (6th and
7th, William IV., chap. 11) provides that "all
masters of vessels coming from foreign ports shall
declare what aliens are on board or have been
landed." It further requires that all aliens on their
arrival from abroad shall declare their name and
description. This declaration it is the duty of the
officer of customs to register, and to transmit a copy
of it to one of the principal Secretaries of State. The
object of the Act, as explained by Lord John Russell
when introducing the bill, was not to impose any restrictions on foreigners, but merely to enable the
Government to ascertain how many foreigners were
in the kingdom at any one time. "It was," said
Lord John, "far less vexatious to require a man
entering this country to say where he came from, and
where he was going to, than to be knocking at a
person's door, and taking a census of his whole
family." Unfortunately, the intention of the author
of the Act has not been carried out in practice. An
inspection of the form of report which the master has
to make, and which is set out in the schedule to the

Customs Law Consolidation Act, 1876, shows that the master is not required to state *where the alien intends to go,* and that all he has to report is the number of alien passengers on board. Moreover, the practice of numbering aliens under the Act soon fell into general disuse. During the last two years indeed, the Customs House authorities have been making an effort to revive it, but the lists are still very imperfect, and cannot be relied on for statistical purposes. The inquiry should be conducted in much more stringent fashion. The master's report should give full particulars, not only of the number of the alien passengers in his ship, but of their nationality, occupation, and destination. This information, however, need only be procured in the case of the great immigrant ships which put in at Hull, Harwich, and Tilbury. No inconvenience need be inflicted on the rest of the continental traffic. The American arrangements for inspection of immigrants are very complete, and may serve as a useful guide. Every immigrant ship is visited six miles from the port of New York by officers of health, and any who may be sick and diseased are removed to hospitals under the care of the Commissioners of Emigration or the Quarantine Commissioners. The others are landed at Castle Garden, where there is a large rotunda capable of accommodating 4,000 persons. Inside this depôt the immediate wants of the immigrants are supplied, special care being taken to prevent their falling into bad hands and being victimised by the crimps.

Once we are satisfied that there is a case for State interference, it is easy to suggest ways of keeping the pauper alien from our shores. The indirect method is to make the domestic workshop amenable to State inspection, and so bring the sweater's den (the only industrial opening which awaits the pauper on his first arrival here) within the reach of the penal law. The Factory and Workshop Bill now before Parliament seeks to accomplish this desirable object, and we wish it Godspeed. The direct method is to pass an **Alien Exclusion Act,** adapted from the legislation of the United States, abstracted at the end of this paper, so as to suit the special circumstances. The indirect benefits flowing from such a measure would be hardly less than the direct. For long before its prohibitory clauses were enforced, it would have checked the operations of the traffickers in human flesh and blood who are at present pursuing that nefarious trade for their own pecuniary ends.

Hostile critics, and there will be such, must not charge us with exaggeration, for we have been careful rather to understate than to overstate the case. Nor do we suppose that we have done more than touch the fringe of the population problem. The lively discussion on the Polish Jew which has been going on in public for the last few weeks, valuable as it

has been on its own account, has been more so for
the reflections to which it has given rise. Men are
beginning to see that the present discontent can only
be partially healed by endeavours on the part of the
New Unionism to organize the unskilled workers,
or by the "Fabian" policy of an eight-hours day.
The true remedy must, it is felt, come in the long run
from within. State-aided and State-enforced education have already done much for the vast multitudes
whose stock-in-trade is the labour of their hands. But
it has yet much to do. It has to impress on the toiling
millions those elementary economic laws, without the
knowledge and observance of which it is hopeless to
expect that their material prospects can be perma-
nently improved. In vain does the Social Democratic Federation insist that the State ought to cap-
ture the land, the mill, and every other instrument of
production, if we are to assume that the numbers who
will share in the fruits of all this State-owned capital
are liable to be indefinitely added to. Get rid of the
struggle for existence to-morrow, and provided this
assumption holds, the last state of this country would
in a few decades have become worse than the first.

Self-respect and self-control are two mainstays of
human happiness, and where these qualities are wanting no State redistribution of worldly goods can per-
manently benefit mankind. That end will best be
compassed by less lofty methods. Abstention from

F

improvident marriages, and from immoderately large families, has, we repeat, long been practised by all possessors of property, and by the more intelligent of our artisans. Moral, just, and reasonable in itself, there is still one class with which it has hitherto failed to find favour—namely, the unskilled and unendowed masses, whose low industrial condition is a barrier to their upward progress. These, unhappily, are just the men to whom the modern theories of social plunder are preached with most effect. It would be well if these preachers, instead of stimulating the predatory instincts of their audience, were to insist now and then on the obvious truth that no one who is labouring hard to gain a competency should habitually act as if he had nothing to lose. The gospel of moderation is not only for the rich. It has to be proclaimed to the poor also. All classes alike must be taught to recognise the fact that the brute creation alone is without responsibility in this matter — without responsibility because without reason.

Here, then, is a field of missionary labour upon which those who have the interests of humanity at heart may be invited to enter boldly. The work is of great and pressing importance. We commend it especially to the energetic followers of Karl Marx and Henry George, who rank, in Hyde Park and elsewhere, as prophets and guides of THE PEOPLE.

APPENDIX (*see* pp. 49 and 64).

I.

An Act approved by Congress to prohibit the importation and migration of foreigners and aliens under contract or agreement to perform labour in the United States of America, Feb. 26th, 1885.

SECTION 1.—It is unlawful for any person, company, etc., in any manner to prepay the transportation, or in any way to assist or encourage the importation or migration, of foreigners and aliens under contract or agreement to perform labour made previous to the importation or migration.

SECTION 2.—Provides that all agreements, etc., made between people to perform labour, etc., in the United States of America shall be void.

SECTION 3.—The penalty for each violation of Section 1 is a fine of 1,000 dollars for each and every offence.

SECTION 4.—Any master of a vessel knowingly bringing any such immigrant labourer into the United States of America is guilty of a misdemeanour, and will be fined 500 dollars for each labourer or 6 months imprisonment or both.

SECTION 5.—Foreigners living temporarily in the United States of America may engage other foreigners as private secretaries, servants, etc. Skilled workmen may be engaged to carry out any new industry which is not already established in the. United States of America.

II.

An Act approved by Congress, Feb. 23rd, 1887, to amend the Act of Feb. 26th, 1885 :—

SECTION 6 (added to the above Act).—Provides for the
examination of ships and for the non-landing of prohibited persons.

SECTION 8.—Prohibited persons are to be returned by any
Boards of Charities which may be designated by the
Secretary of the Treasury, which Board shall be com-
pensated by Government.

The expense of return to be borne by the owners of
vessels bringing such prohibited persons; vessels refusing to pay such expenses shall not land at nor clear
from any port.

III.

An Act to prohibit the importation or migration of
foreigners or aliens, which was approved by Congress
of the United States on March 3rd, 1891.

SECTION 1.—The following classes of aliens shall be excluded from admission into the United States in
accordance with the existing Acts regulating immigration other than those concerning Chinese
labourers :—

All idiots, insane persons, paupers or persons who are
likely to become a public charge, persons suffering
from a loathsome or contagious disease, persons who
have been convicted of a felony or infamous crime or
misdemeanour involving moral turpitude, polygamists,
and any other persons whose tickets or passages have
been paid for with the money of others or who are
assisted to come by others, unless it is affirmatively
and satisfactorily shown on special inquiry that such
person does not belong to one of the foregoing excluded classes or contract labourers excluded by the
Act of Feb. 26th, 1885. But this section does not pre-
clude persons living in the United States from sending

out for a relative or friend who is not one of the excluded classes.

And the Act is not construed to apply to exclude persons
convicted of a political offence.

SECTION 3.—It is a violation of the Act of Feb. 26th, 1885,
to assist or encourage importation or migration of any
alien by promises of employment through advertisements printed and published in any foreign country;
and any alien coming to the United States in consequence of such advertisement shall be treated as
coming under a contract as contemplated by such
Act.

SECTION 4.—No steamship company or owners of vessels
shall directly or through their agents, either by
writing, printing, or oral representations, solicit,
invite, or encourage the immigration of any alien
into the United States of America, except by ordinary
letters, circulars, and advertisements, or oral representations, stating the sailing of their vessels and
terms and facilities of transportation therein.

Penalty under this section is a fine of 1,000 dollars for
every offence.

SECTION 6.—Any person who brings or lands in the United
States of America by vessel or otherwise, or who shall
aid any alien not lawfully entitled to land, shall be
fined 1,000 dollars or one year's imprisonment or both.

SECTION 8.—Captains of vessels must give the name,
nationality, last residence, and destination of each
alien before landing. They will be inspected on board.

SECTION 10.—All aliens who unlawfully come into the
United States of America shall, if practicable, be immediately sent back on the vessel by which they were
brought; the cost of maintenance on land and the
expense of their return shall be borne by the owners
of the vessels on which the aliens came; if the owner,
master, agent, or consignee shall refuse or neglect to

return them to the port from which they came he shall be fined 300 dollars for each and every offence, and the vessel shall have no clearance from any port till the fine is paid.

SECTION 11.—Aliens can be returned within one year at the expense of the owners of the vessel bringing them; if that cannot be done, then they are to be returned at Government expense. Any alien who becomes a public charge within one year after arrival, from causes existing prior to his landing, will be returned.

THE MORAL ASPECT.

By the Rev. G. S. Reaney.

No apology is needed for the inclusion in this *symposium* of a short essay upon the moral aspects of ALIEN PAUPER IMMIGRATION. The ethical side of all public questions looms large at the present moment. Political partisanship and political economy have their place, doubtless, amongst the forces and facts of our very complex national life; and it were most foolish for any one who thinks, writes, or works, in regard to what are called "the problems of the day," to ignore such potent influences. But, on the other hand, the "moral side" of all things with which this restless age concerns itself must not, cannot, be ignored. The fiercest political partisans may rave and rant at the "fanatics," as they are pleased to dub the "Moralists"; and the driest and most indifferent "economists" may add their less irate contribution to the blatant abuse so largely poured out, in the press and on platforms, upon the men who give conscience the first place in public affairs: yet the fact remains, beyond dispute, that the English people will not consider such questions as the "state of the poor" apart from their moral bearings and ethical issues. So deeply indeed has this "higher aspect" of all public and national affairs forced itself into the common mind, that it has become a powerful factor in both political and commercial life. The "character of political leaders," and the "conditions of labour," are no mere sentimental sentences, culled from the random rhetoric of excited philanthropists; they are sober words, full of force and meaning, and big with practical results in the two worlds of statesmanship and trade.

The subject which has given the occasion for, and forms the matter of, this book is a part of the larger question, "the state of the poor." That question, in its broad outlines, has filled a big place in the press, and in the public mind and imagination, during the last few years, and it has forced its way to the front of all political, social, and religious discussions. At first it looked so large, and presented such enormous, not to say, monstrous, proportions, that the biggest brains failed to comprehend it, and the most generous hearts failed fully to feel it. But with the practical good sense and the real sympathy so characteristic of the English people, the great problem is now in the course of being taken to pieces and considered in detail; and as the result of that sensible endeavour to master the matter, the "immigration of pauper aliens" has been made the subject of official inquiry, and bids fair to become one of the questions which, in the near future, will engage the attention of Parliament.

In order to understand the moral bearings of the subject of Alien Immigration, it will be needful, in the first place, that we recall to our minds some indisputable facts connected with the condition of the poor in the great cities and centres of England. Much has, doubtless, been said in regard to the poor, which has erred on the side of rhetoric and sentiment. Poverty, in all ages and in all countries, has been the shadow of riches. In an age phenomenally wealthy, and in cities splendidly rich, poverty is sure to be found; and, by the law of contrast, its miseries and its sins will seem more deeply dark and more densely sad, because of the "life of wealth" with which it lies in close contiguity, and with which it compares with an intensity that nothing seems to mitigate or hide. But in the interest of those for whom these pages are written, it is of first importance that there be no indulgence in exaggeration, and no overstatement of fact. For such exaggeration there is no need, and for such overstatement of fact there is little opportunity. Writers upon "the poverty" and the "East Ends" of our great cities are under no necessity to do more than let the light of verification fall upon the dark alleys, the dirty streets, the overcrowded "homes" (!) and the laborious and sorrowful life of the city poor, to prove that a condition of things exists that calls for careful, vigorous, and practical treatment at the hands of Parliament, and at the cost of the English people.

Let the normal state of many a city "East End" be remembered. Poverty is there—whatever be its cause—poverty of work, of wages, of comfort, of resource, of opportunity, of character, and of life. I will not attempt to describe it. But a most truthful, yet restrained description of the condition of the "poor" of many a city is given in the report of the "Sweating Committee" (1890, p. cxxxv), in which the "inefficiency of the workers, early marriages, and the tendency of the residuum of the population in large towns to form a helpless community, together with a low standard of life, and the excessive supply of "unskilled labour," are said to be the chief "factors in producing sweating." No more accurate description of the cities of the poorest of the poor could be penned. But let it be not be forgotten that the poor, of which this description is given, are just those into whose midst in London, Leeds, Manchester, etc., the turbid streams of alien pauper immigration are constantly flowing, deepening and broadening the area of that community which, in the expressive words of the Sweating Committee's report is "helpless"! We start with a condition of things as miserable as it is menacing. And yet into that area of "helplessness"

we permit to pass every day a dirty, alien, and yet
more helpless inflow of humanity, coming from the
far off cities of Russia, Hungary, and Poland; and
bringing with it poverty, ignorance, and the vices
common to the deeper depths of continental cities!

On the face of it, it looks as if the practice of *laisser
faire* was not the height of wisdom or the depth of
statesmanship. It might be thought that something
could be suggested to remedy a state of things for
which the most profound political, economic, and
moral justification must be found, if it is to continue
after the revelations made of late before Parliamentary
Committees as to the condition of the poor in those
parts of London, Leeds, and Manchester to which
the alien pauper immigrants come by hundreds, and
under the force of attractions which, when once
understood, make their advent both a mystery and an
addition to the misery already too prevalent in the
East Ends of great cities.

I know it will be said, "There has been inquiry,
and one result of that inquiry is set forth in a
sentence in the report of the Committee on Sweating,
in which the opinion is stated that too much stress
had been laid upon the injurious effects on wages
caused by foreign immigration." But let it be added
that farther on in the report this statement is somewhat modified, and we learn that certain trades are
undoubtedly affected by the presence of poor for-

cigners. Now if trades be affected, all else is affected
—sanitation, social habits, home life, manners, and
morals. The normal condition of large areas of
English cities is sad enough and bad enough. All
the moral evils that follow poverty, overcrowding,
physical depression, the fierce temptation to the over-
tried and helpless of vice, drink, and idleness, are there
with a breadth and a depth that make good men
despair and bad men grow cynical. So deeply is it felt
that the "conditions of life" in city East Ends must
be bettered before the people will be "better," that
strenuous efforts are made to "lift" men and women
out of these "submerged areas" into happier conditions, where decency is possible, and where life may
find a fairer chance of being worth the living, and
childhood may be sweet, love pure, and humanity
human.

Yet, how strange! down at the "Docks" there
may be seen a crowd of emigrants standing on the
deck of some outward-bound steamer, and looking
their last farewell—half sad and half glad—to their
old home and fatherland, and steaming away to the
West, where they may begin again, under brighter conditions, "life's fight that is ever fierce," but, while
fierce, need not always fail. And then, yet more
strange! just on the other side of the "Dock" there
pours out from the decks of some continental ship
a bigger mass of alien, dirty, miserable immigrants,

brought over to crowd into the very cities, streets, workshops and houses from which the emigrants have just steamed away. Now this anomaly, strange as it seems, goes on weekly. It has its economic side, and it has its moral parable. At home we want more room, more air, more work, more wages, and more decent houses. We can only get much of this by emigration. And yet side by side with emigration is this immigration, making the physical, trade, social, and moral conditions of our cities graver, more menacing, and more difficult in every sense. On all hands we hear the cry from the city to the country folk, " Don't come up ; we are too many." And every worker in city slums knows right well that they are too many for health, for wages, for honest work, for home life, for childhood, for decency, for chastity and faith. And yet we are to stand aside, and let the alien pauper in—with all that he carries on his face, in his clothes, and in his person ; ay, let him in with a hearty welcome from the sentimentalist and the capitalist !

Were not another word written, this seems plain. On moral grounds, with *prima facie* evidence of the character, aims, and habits of the alien pauper immigrant, he is just the one person who ought not to be admitted to bring himself, his belongings, his poverty, and his habits into the overcrowded East Ends of English cities and towns.

But we are met at once with the rejoinder, "The
alien pauper immigrant is the modern political and
religious refugee to whom England has always given a
welcome, protection, and a home." The moral argument, we are told, is all in favour of our alien friend.
Of course this statement is made with perfect good
faith. Now, whatever it is worth, it is somewhat
limited in the area of its influence. The political
refugee and the religious exile are chiefly Semitics,
driven out of Russia, and perhaps in a few cases
exiled from Germany. If it is demanded of those
who oppose the present method and manner of alien
immigration that they give up contending for its
modification, restraint, and, in some phases of it
cessation, just because some one says that the Jews
are being expelled from Russia because they are
Jews, and on grounds purely political and religious,
it is but natural that we should ask for some very
definite proof of that statement. With the most
profound appreciation of the ability of "our own
correspondent," it is asking too much that the alien
pauper shall be allowed to " come in his thousands,"
on the bare statement made by himself, his co-
religionists, and gentlemen of the press, often hard up
for good copy, that he is a political exile or a religious
refugee ! Certainly England has aforetime welcomed
the victims of Spanish persecution, of French religious
bigotry, and in doing so she has in trade, in liberty,

and in faith received an ample reward. The people
who crowd Hatton Garden, swarm in Soho, and
possess the very "gate of their enemies" in Whitechapel, may be men to whom the sale of horrible
spirits to the Russian peasants, the lending of money
on monstrous usury, and the gradual and utter de-
moralization of thousands of Russian communes are
things quite unknown; but before we are prepared
to receive the motley multitude that comes from over
the sea, and across the vast plains of Russia, with
open arms, as political exiles, and as religious
refugees, suffering for high, noble, and exalted
virtues, for faithfulness to the faith of their fathers
and to their God, we must know more about them,
and we must assure ourselves that the only reason
for their expulsion from Russia is because they are
so pure and saintly and true to the best traditions of
the remarkable race to which they belong.

Further. Before Englishmen are asked to accept
the very lofty character given to these immigrants,
it might surely be granted that some such estimate
should, ere this, have been formed concerning them
by their co-religionists, both on the Continent and in
England. The great Semitic race includes within its
unique area the poorest and the richest, the alien
pauper and the naturalized millionaire. Now no one
can say that any very remarkable excitement or
action has taken place amongst the big people of

modern Israel in regard to the persecution in Russia and elsewhere of their poor brethren. If the persecution has been real, if it has been because of the Israelite religion, and if it has been as severe and undeserved as we are told it is, why, in the name of "kith and kin," "faith and fathers," have not the emperors of the European bourses brought the for ever borrowing emperor of the North to book? If these immigrants are political exiles or religious refugees, it is rather hard upon the poor of Whitechapel that they are to make room for them to come in, and make the fight for bread fiercer in order that these hungry and hunted Semities may find house, home and liberty in England. Why have not the big-pursed men, who hold the secret, not of all the creeds, but of all the stock-markets and borrowing houses in Europe, played a nobler part, and brought the persecuting Czar to his marrow-bones, and so saved the exile and the refugee from his long flight and sad escape from political tyranny to find himself the slave of the East End sweater?

There is ample justification for the use of much salt in regard to the whole story of the interesting but not overclean "political exiles," and the uncouth and not over devout "religious refugees" from which the East End of London suffers so much.

But supposing that the lot of the alien pauper when at home is hard, does it follow that it is playing the part of a friend to him to entice or welcome him to the East End of London, or to Strangeways in Manchester? This is a question of the highest morality, for it appeals in no sense either to our fears or our hopes. It is put purely in the interest of the alien himself. Of course it may be said, "No one entices these immigrants. They come, and we feel bound to welcome them when they come." It is not the place to discuss the means and methods by which the pauper foreigners are attracted to our shores. A full inquiry might however disclose some remarkable facts. Let that pass. Would it not be kind to let the pilgrims of the new exodus know what sort of "promised land" awaits them here? Nay, might it not be even more kind to make the path of that pilgrimage more difficult, not to say impassable? Will some of the readers of this book take a stroll in Hatton Garden, Soho, Whitechapel, and some of the slums of Manchester? And let such think of men, women, and children brought over in scores and hundreds, and just pitched down in an alien land, ignorant of its language, ignorant of its trade customs, wages, work, civic rights, and religion, and left to make the best of it under conditions intolerable to the native-born Englishman. There is no need to accept the rhetorical description of the Paris correspondent of the *Times* about a Sunday slave-market in Whitechapel. But there is need to

G

read the pages of the evidence laid before the Sweating Committee as to the conditions of life to the
"Greener" down East. There is need to go and
see for oneself what life is behind Aldgate, in Bethnal Green, and where the Semitic face pushes out
the "flat-nosed" Saxon, and the weird names of Hebrew sound and foreign phrase spread themselves
street by street in Whitechapel, and the language of
the pavement is not even the English oath or the
brutal Cockney jest, but a speech that comes from over
the sea. Before we hear so much about the "exile's
home" and the "refugee's refuge," it might be well
to know what sort of a haven they will find who
seek our shores. There are moments, it must be
admitted, when those who live and labour in the great
East End feel hot and angry at the sight of the faces
so un-English, and the sound of the speech so utterly
foreign, which crowd pavement and road on Whitechapel waste, about the Minories, and all away down
Commercial Street and Bethnal Green. But anger
soon passes into pity when the thought comes into the
heart—the thought of these poor wretches, landless,
homeless, and helpless — the victims of imperial
tyranny, say some, of their own wrong-doing and
greed, say others—for years the victims of trade customs so cruel, of sweating so brutal, and of circumstance and social conditions so debasing, that the
only thing in their life that makes it bearable is

the companionship of thousands like unto themselves.

If these men and women are political exiles and
religious refugees, and we, in England, are bound in
conscience, in faith, and in fealty to the splendid tradition of our freedom and our power, to give them
protection, safety and home, then let us do it, as in
the sight of God, with some thoughtfulness, some
wisdom, and some care. It is the sheerest hypocrisy
in the world for any one to talk of "protecting the
political exile from imperial wrath, and of guarding
the religious refugee from the bigotry of an ignorant
Greek priesthood," when all that we do is to let these
exiles and refugees crowd into the dense, dark,
debased and horrible areas of our city East Ends!
Do the defenders of this cheap heroism realize what it
all means to the very poor wretches over whom they
are so sweetly sentimental and so selfishly indifferent?
Let such "defenders of England's noble name" take
a lodging down in Whitechapel; let them spend days
and weeks in studying the "labour market," the
"lodging-houses," the "food markets," the clothes
fairs, the Semitic Sundays, and the "sweater's shop."
The result will be everything but agreeable to the
amour propre of these friends of the exile and the
refugee. *The brickfields of Egypt must have been
pleasant compared with* the cellars, garrets, shops,
and so-called factories in which the miserable alien
pauper lives out his sad, toilsome, hopeless life.

Of course they are not slaves! They can sell their
labour and, if need be, their life, on the best terms
they can get! They are, in a sense, amongst their
own people! Yes; but it is possible that they find
little comfort in that fact. The worst "sweaters"
at the East End are prosperous "exiles" and "refugees." For even the best of them there is little in
their life calculated to lift them, reform them, or better
them. They never assimilate our habits or become
Englishmen. In face, instinct, language and character their children are aliens, and still exiles. They
seldom really become citizens; and our code of morality they never get by heart, but our vices they learn.
As they come, so they remain—aliens, children of
another race, amongst us, yet not of us. And the
East End produces no type of man or woman so
unfit, un-English, and morally and personally so alien,
as the pauper immigrant when he becomes a settler
in the regions of Hatton Garden, Soho, and the
East End. If, when he comes amongst us, he is a
political patriot, exiled for his sturdy independence
and honest speech, or a religious refugee, driven from
the land of his fathers by cruel laws and edicts for
the crime of which Daniel and the three Hebrew
youths were condemned, it is certain that the haven
of safety and the home of liberty to which he has been
welcomed have served him but ill; for it needs only a
few years of life amongst us to turn the political exile

into the dreariest drudge of the sweater, without one
political idea or hope, and to change the present religious refugee into a poor slave of toil who knows no
Sabbath, feels no inspiration in the splendid psalms
and prophecies of his fathers, and finds no hope even
in the unutterable name of his God.

If we are to welcome these alien paupers as exiles
and refugees, victims of a brutal tyranny, let us do
our duty with them, and save them from physical,
social and moral conditions which make their last lot
worse than their first, and life in England less to be
desired than life in the communes of Russia and the
cities of Southern Europe.

There remains a yet more serious aspect of Alien
Pauper Immigration. What are its moral effects upon
our own people in those localities into which the in-
comers crowd ?

Sufficient evidence has been set forth in other chap-
ters of this book to make it allowable for me to
accept many facts as proved. In the first part of this
essay I showed from the report of the " Sweating "
and the " Emigration and Immigration " Committees,
that the normal condition of thousands of the poor
was, to use the word already quoted, "helpless." To
allow, and even encourage, the immigration of alien
paupers into such areas, where such conditions prevail,
is, on the face of it, perilous in the extreme. It is
quite impossible to traverse the whole breadth of the

facts brought out in the two inquiries referred to, and substantiated most fully by independent research and testimony. At the best, in London, Leeds, Manchester, and all large towns, *there are thousands of people to whom life is one grave, anxious, troubled thought!* Work, for some reason, is always irregular, wages fluctuating and low, houses difficult to obtain or miserable to live in, and health precarious, and the bright things of the world few or unknown.

During many years of close observation it was forced upon my mind that *the chronic condition of tens of thousands of the poor is that of a ceaseless and almost unvarying depression.* It comes from many causes. It is an heredity, the heritage of generations of overwork and under pay. It is a social condition occasioned by want of food, the uncertainty of employment, sickness, the fear of long illness, of the workhouse, and of a pauper's funeral and grave. It comes also from bad air, insanitation, overcrowding, drink, and the awful monotony of daily life. In the East End this "depression" has become quite a symptom of the common lot of thousands. It looks out of the face of the poor in streets, in the trams, in the workshops, and in their homes.

> "Mostly men's many-featured faces wear
> Looks of fixed gloom, or else of restless care;
> The very babes, that in their cradles lie,
> Out of the depths of unknown troubles cry."

This "depression" is very wide and deep amongst the East End poor. I feel sure that the presence of the alien pauper increases it immensely. The sight of one Semitic face seemed to act as a damper upon the spirits of men and women who met the keen competition of their fellow countrymen as a natural thing. But when visiting the poor when times were bad, I often heard the weary complaint, "It's them Jews." Time after time have I heard that lament. Many men and women, struggling to keep a home over their heads, but driven out of work by the foreigner, who *could* "live on less," and who *would* take less, and work *longer*, have said to me, "What's the use? the Jews are coming by thousands, and there will be nothing left." I know it has been said that the Gentile has gone to the wall because he flies to the "pub" more than the Jew. There are such cases, but my own experience does not justify the sweeping statement made by Miss Potter before the Sweating Committee. "The Gentile makes money to drink, the Jews to save." The coming of the alien pauper has, I feel sure, a most depressing effect upon thousands of English men and women, both in London and Manchester. I write from what I have heard and seen.

Now, if there is one thing we want to bring about amongst the poor, it is hope. But the presence, especially in London, of thousands of foreign-faced men and women crowding into the dense parts of the

poorer quarters of the great city does not so much anger
our own people as it saddens them. Quite apart from
other questions, their alien looks, habits and language,
combined with their remarkable fecundity, tenacity
and money-getting gift, make them a ceaseless weight
upon the poor amongst whom they live. The marvel
is that the depression has not turned to anger, and
that we have not had a "Jew-hunt," such as has
been known abroad. May it never come! but many
things are more improbable. Not anger with the
alien pauper, but a kind of pathetic sadness at the
hardness of his own lot, seems to possess the minds of
thousands of the poor in our big city, who feel the
Semitic alien both a burden and a fear.

The moral results of this daily depression are seen
on all hands. Many give up the fight in despair, or
turn to the solace of drink, or even to the deadly
diversion of cheap vice ! People who go occasionally
to the East End may fail to realize these facts ; but to
those who have lived in its streets, and amongst its
people, the frightful depression, hopelessness, and
despair of thousands of the poor is the most difficult
factor in their sad lives. It is a foolish policy to
deepen that depression by permitting the incoming
of hundreds of alien people, poorer than the poor,
yet able and willing to live under conditions which
are bearable only to Englishmen who have given up
all hope and self-help, and who drift from street to

street, from house to house, and from job to job, until
death seems life's most blessed expectation. And yet
such is the patient policy pursued by our authorities
at the present hour in regard to the immigration of
the pauper aliens.

*The pauper alien intensifies the keen competition,
always too fierce, in the labour market.* That such is
the fact has been more than proved over and over
again. There is no need to do more than restate
it. But one or two illustrations of its method and
influence upon the moral life of the poor may be
ad rem. Only those who have watched the ways
of the " Sweater " can understand how that a comparatively small number of men and women can bring
down the prices of work in the over-crowded East
Ends of our cities of the poor. It does not require
a thousand " seekers after work " to take off a half-
penny or even a penny in the dozen for articles in
the making of which the alien is a keen competitor
with English men and women. Such a scene as this
is not unknown down East. A crowd of seekers
after work. One woman goes into the office, or workshop, or warehouse. She is starving, or what is,
in its effect, equally bad, she is fairly well to do,
but wants to make a little pocket-money, or to lay
up a small fund for a " trip." Any way she is prepared to take what she can get. The keen buyer
of her labour soon finds her out, and beats her down,

little by little, until she accepts, as is often the case when she is not in absolute need of the work, such a price as her more necessitous sisters cannot live upon. But that price rules the market for the day, and the fairly well-to-do woman, wanting to earn a little sum for herself, robs the mother, the lonely widow, or the solitary woman of what would have been a better payment for her work. That affects not one, but scores, and in some cases, hundreds. Let the one case be multiplied by scores; let the hungry, eager, able-to-live-almost-upon-nothing alien come in, crowd into the labour market of London or Manchester, and the result is self-evident. The "sweater" becomes master of the situation, and the poor half-fed, over-worked man or woman the victim.

Now the economic effects of such competition are not within the scope of this essay, only so far as they have moral results; and they have very terrible results upon the home, the character, and the tone of the life of the poor.

Lower wages, irregularity in work, with spells of idleness and spells of over-work, have very certain moral results. Nothing so soon breaks down the moral nerve of a man as keen competition, followed by a smaller wage, irregular employment, with the necessity for cheaper lodgings, cheaper food, a cheaper life all round. It just takes the heart out of a man. But it may be said, and justly said, "This effect

comes of all competition." It does. There is nothing
singular in the fact that the influx of hundreds
of pauper aliens into the labour market of London,
Leeds, and Manchester brings with it all the evils of
over-competition. That must be admitted. It might
be a boon if the fact were singular. It does not
seem to show that the policy of letting things alone
is wise, because the immigrants from Russia only
intensify a condition of things too prevalent in all big
centres of population already. But there is an aspect,
a moral aspect, to this competition, so far as the
alien pauper is concerned, which is somewhat singular
and unique. It is this. The alien, notwithstanding
many virtues, seems to bring a sort of social contagion with him, which has the effect of seriously
deteriorating the life of those of our own people who
are compelled to be his neighbour. It is a painful
thing to write, but truth compels the statement, that
wherever the foreigner comes in any number, the
neighbourhood in which he settles speedily drops in
tone, in character, and in morals. It can be seen
most distinctly in those districts in London where
the alien is to be found in large numbers. The same
fact is patent in regard to any trade into which the
alien enters in any considerable force. It is a fact
which soon makes itself felt, and those who watch
the steady and almost stealthy spreading of certain
importations from abroad in London and Manchester

can quite confirm the statement. It is something
very subtle and strange. It may not be possible for
any one to say "they drink" or "their life is filled
with lubricity," yet it seems to have a lowering influence upon the manners and the morals of all who
are compelled to herd with the foreigner. Their very
virtues seem prolific of evil when, like some seed
blown by the winds, they fall and fructify in English
soil. It may be difficult to explain the fact, but
fact it is. The statement of it may give offence in
some quarters. That is to be regretted. But the
existence of the fact is an offence, and a grave offence,
in our city life and in our national morals. It is
a very serious thing to know that in the East End,
and in other parts of London and certain well-known
cities, this contagion in the life of the poorest of the
poor spreads apace, increasing year by year in its
fatal force, and forming one of the saddest factors
in the poverty of thousands. Surely it belongs to
us as a nation to consider this sincerely and earnestly.
Mr. Tillett's account of five hundred emigrants departing from the Docks, driven out of England by the
pressure of over-crowded life, while, at the same hour,
and near the same spot, seven hundred pauper aliens
were coming in, has all the elements of tragedy and
comedy. But it can easily be surpassed, in that
respect, by the equally true statement, that while in
the East End we send hundreds of earnest workers,

and spend thousands of pounds in an endeavour to
drive out sadness, over-work, sorrow, and sin, we do
our best to defeat our philanthropic purpose by permitting the incoming of the alien pauper, who deepens
sadness, increases weariness, spoils much work, and
spreads a peculiar influence amongst the poor, utterly
inimical to home life, to honest toil, to fair work, to
fair wage, and to Sabbath keeping, and destructive of
that faith and character without which the lifting of
city East Ends is a hopeless task.

Two grave facts have been set forth in this essay.
The alien pauper deepens the awful depression which
rests upon the life of the poor, especially in the East
End of London, in some parts of Manchester, and
other towns. Further, the alien immigrant spreads a
sort of contagion in all neighbourhoods where he
settles in any considerable number, and through any
trade upon which he lays his hands. It may be said
that these statements are vague and incapable of
actual proof. They are vague, I admit, when put side
by side with figures and physical facts; but that
vagueness belongs to all morals when considered in
connection with what may be called the mechanics of
life. But let any one who has worked and lived east
of Aldgate Pump consider the two points I have
sought to emphasize and illustrate, and I feel sure that
the conviction will force itself into his mind that I
have not written about mere imaginary things or the

creations of my own fancy. Every clergyman and
minister, every city missionary, every schoolmaster,
and every worker in the East End and in the slums of
great cities, knows perfectly well that the two prime
necessities of all social reform are Hope and Health.
Who has not, when working amongst the poor, longed
for something that would rouse them from their apathy,
and lift them out of their depression? Who has not
learnt that in every strike, with all its necessary sorrow
and evil, there is a splendid force for stirring thousands into mental exertion, and for quickening hope
and effort in the heart and life of men often too
dull to care for anything beyond something to drink.
Now to such, the influx, especially into London, of
the ever-coming, ever-increasing, the ever-competing
pauper alien is a fact big with the saddest results to
tens of thousands in the suffocating streets of the
East End. It means that work will be less, wages
lower, houses dearer, competition more keen, and life
more dull, dark, and depressing. Let it be imagined
for a moment that the "open door" through which the
alien enters were closed. Let it further be imagined
that the splendid scheme with which Baron Hirsch is
credited had come to a practical realization, and that in
London a new exodus had set in under the guidance
of the modern Moses, and that thousands of the race
that spoiled the Egyptians journeyed down the broad
streets that lead to the Docks at Poplar—what would

be the effect upon the poor in Whitechapel, Bethnal
Green, and St. George's-in-the-East? Immense. I
could believe that in thousands of hearts of London's
poor the thought would kindle like a new-born hope,
"We shall have a chance now!" That thought would
be an inspiration and a help. But I fear the suggestion is only a dream of a dream. Every day sees them
come, and every week only adds to their numbers. The
"crowd of life" gets more crowded, the competition
becomes more keen, the poverty deeper, the sorrow
more hopeless, and the common life of the poor more
helpless. Nothing is done save a feeble and fussy
effort to count the aliens who land at the Docks or
come by more stealthy ways into the city. Never did
the good people of all creeds so earnestly care for the
poor, seek their betterment and their social salvation.
But, side by side with all their efforts, there is an
influence, powerful, prevalent, and in ceaseless living
activity, which is foreign in character, apart in habit,
lacking all those fibrous characteristics which, even
amongst the worst of our people, help to keep men a
little manly and women somewhat chaste; an influence that increases in force every day, that is fiercely
competitive in labour, unsocial, unpatriotic, because it
hath no real citizenship amongst us, and altogether
antagonistic to our common faith, and unsympathetic
towards all our highest ideals and noblest aims; an
influence which lies upon the life of thousands of the

poorest of the poor like a burden, and penetrates that
life with forces such as no English Christian can con-
template unmoved; an influence that is amongst us by
our own permission, and is not a growth of our own
soil, but an importation. What is the duty of Government, of Parliament, and of the Nation? To let this
thing alone? To leave the door still open? To stand
alone amidst the nations of the world, permitting anything to make its home where there is least room for
it, and least moral and physical resources calculated to
master it, mould it, and make it into a peaceful factor
towards all that is best in our national life? Is that
the duty of a representative Government, supposed to
exist for the greatest good of the greatest number?

The policy of "let alone" is pretty well played out,
and gone with the brutal doctrine of the "survival of
the fittest." It has played its part of an implacable
indifference long enough. Governments must govern,
or the people will. Of course it will be said the alien
pauper is "a good deal of a bogey," and we shall once
again be enjoined not to "talk about heroic remedies"
until we have ascertained that we have a really dangerous disease to deal with. But all that sort of
"arm-chair" criticism goes for little in face of the
facts which every day makes more palpable in regard
to the pressure of the alien immigration upon the very
poor of East London and elsewhere. As for the much
higher criticism of the " political exile and the religious

refugee" sort, that has pretty well had its day. It
starts with a great assumption, scarcely sustained by
facts. It lays upon the poor of the East End a
responsibility which surely belongs in the first place
to the co-religionists and the co-patriots of these persecuted people; and it takes up with a fussy osten-
tation the case of exiles and refugees who, if they
deserve any care and sympathy as such, ought not to
be left by the lofty-minded defenders of modern
Huguenots to find a haven of rest in Whitechapel, and
a home in the arms of the sweater!

If it is the duty of England to open her ports and
her cities to these immigrants, it must be equally her
duty to see that, when they come, they shall find
something more suitable to political patriots than an
East End slum, and something more conducive to the
better exercise of their religious convictions than
the horrible physical and social conditions under the
influence of which, poor, alone, and often betrayed
by false friends, they drift from street to street and
from sweater to sweater, until they become the most
hopeless and helpless of the deepest residuum of a
great city.

If, again, prompted by the memory of the days
when the Huguenot found a refuge on our shores,
England stretches out sympathetic arms of welcome
to these "exiles and refugees," it surely becomes her
duty to see, not only that they are "housed" in

H

decency, and treated with honesty and honourable
care, but that her own " sons of toil," fighting in our
big towns for very life, shall not find that fight made
more fierce, and that life made more sad and sinful,
because of the incoming of men and women alien in
race, religion, and character. If it is impossible to
check, divert, or stop the inflow of the alien immigrant ; if he is a must-be of our civilized inter-
nationalism and of our Christianized hospitality ; if he
is one of the very factors of our economic free trade,
—surely, by every consideration capable of realization
by a nation so generous and so noble, our own fellow
citizens, our own brothers and sisters after the flesh,
ought, with equal sympathy and with yet more than
equal Christian love, to be guarded from evils which
even a child might anticipate would arise from the
incoming into our poorer life of thousands of men and
women alien in race, in social habits, and in religion,
and so fiercely competitive in that labour world
wherein our poor have to gain their daily bread, not
only by the sweat of their brow, but often by the
breaking of their heart. By every moral consideration, bearing alike upon the condition, character, and
life of the alien immigrant, as well as upon the state
of our own fellow countrymen, whose misfortune it is
to be poor, overworked, and underpaid, we, as a nation,
are bound to see that, either we shut our ports to
the Russian and foreign refugees, or that their settle-

ment in our midst shall not be inimical to their social progress and moral growth, nor dangerous to the health, happiness, and ethical betterment of our own people.

STATUTORY AND OFFICIAL PROVISIONS.

By C. J. Follett.

"A man must live by his work, and his wages must at least, be sufficient to maintain him."

Thus wrote our great political economist of the last century; and, as a corollary to this, it has been written that " man cannot safely increase in any country beyond the means of subsistence available for his support."

The means of subsistence are not now as they were then. The subsistence of a country is no longer confined to its own produce. Steam, and other means of communication, have made the subsistence of countries the granaries of the world.

At any rate, so long as we keep the seas open, this is so with us. The means of subsistence are with us the power of purchasing them.

The paraphrase of the above quotations should, therefore, now, be that man cannot, with safety, increase in any way so as to make his purchasing power of the means of subsistence no longer available for his support.

What is true of a country generally, is true, mainly,

as to its labouring class, which are the larger portion, and the producers of its wealth; and so it comes to this—that in no country, with safety, can wages be reduced to less than the purchasing power of the means of subsistence.

For a country to be, in this respect, in a thoroughly wholesome position, it should be able to be asserted, as to all its industries, that such a reduction does not occur.

It may, perhaps, be Utopian to expect as much as this, in even the happiest community. But a community falls short of the happiness which it should aspire to attain to, if it can be said that this is markedly not the position in any noticeable portion. If any noticeable portion is condemned, from any cause, to work for less than will give the means of subsistence available for its support, something is at fault which calls for correction.

But then comes the important question, What is subsistence?

This is a varying quantity dependent on the habits of the particular society, acquired by generations; and, also, on climatic and other influences. Mere life is subsistence in some countries and societies; in others life, so reduced, is not worth the having, and its people are entitled, of right, to something better.

Liberal reward of labour is the test of national

wealth, and should be proportioned to that wealth.
With its increase, the habits and mode of life of
the labouring classes become more elevated. They
advance with it ; and they have as much a vested
right to this advance as capital invested has to its
repayment. Improved enjoyment is the interest on
their capital. A brighter life is as much theirs as is
the dividend on money in the National Funds the
property of the inscribed holder.

In a wealthy community, therefore, subsistence of
the labourer means, not only existence, but fair and
reasonable means to enjoy life. He has a right to
this. It is his mode of subsistence ; and if his wages
drag him down below this, he has not got the means
of subsistence ; he is existing without them, and
contrary to the fundamental rules of how man should
exist and increase.

And if this should be largely the case, the injury is
not confined to him alone. Wages are the sum which
the habits of each society render necessary for subsistence according to its customs. If the labouring
class fails to receive these, it will lower, of necessity,
the habits of the larger portion of the community
which they are ; and, with them, it will affect the
habits of the community at large.

With decaying wealth in a community a decay
of wages naturally follows, and want and mortality
are the result. To allow this to occur in a community

where wealth in the aggregate is not decaying, but holds its own, is a blot on the social system.

These are all, I know, only truisms, and very trite; but I venture to name them as leading up to the question at issue.

The question is this : Are we, or are we not, being seriously injured by large importations of foreigners, willing to work, legally, honestly and quietly, it may be, but for considerably less wages than our own people do work for, and, indeed, can work for consistently with our ideas of subsistence? And if we are being so injured, ought we to do anything to stop the injury? And if we ought so to do, what should the particular remedial steps be?

I suppose there are some ardent worshippers of cheapness, who would assert that lowered price of commodities obtained, even at this risk, must be accepted as a blessing, and not resisted.

But is the good thus obtained in any way commensurate with the evil? It takes a wide range, and considerable time, for lowered wages to reduce prices, generally, even if they do it at all. Meanwhile, the suffering and misery are great.

Cheaper trousers and cheaper boots in Brook Street and Bond Street will not add to the necessaries and conveniences of the East End ; and if those necessaries and conveniences fall short, by sharp reduction, of what the habits and proper customs of the people, and the requirements of the climate to those born in it, demand, a grave deterioration must take place in their habits.

This would be sufficiently serious if nothing else was imported except very cheap, even though not dishonest, industry. Unfortunately, however, the cheap industry does not come alone. Its Lares and Penates are certainly at a minimum; but it brings with it a most sinister companion, which largely aggravates the evil.

Cleanliness is mainly an occidental religion, and is not worshipped as much as it should be in the lands of the rising sun. After the visit of Peter the Great to inspect our metropolis, two hundred years ago, the house in which he lodged was so filthy that the especial payment from the Exchequer to clean it is a matter of history. Similar experiences of Oriental visitation have, if rumour be true, been felt in recent years. The inundation of the East End by the poor foreigners who come, with their empty hands and their unsavoury habits, not only reduces the capacity of our own people to resist dirt and degradation, but largely increases the volume of dirt and degradation to be resisted.

An evil somewhat of the same kind has been at the door of Great Britain always, and especially in the last century with its easy sea passage—in the large influx of labour from Ireland.

There was, thence, an influx of sturdy, quick-witted labour, but with considerably lower conceptions of subsistence than in this country, and lower demand for the power to purchase. The introduction of this totally different labour, with lower tastes and habits, would have been a most threatening evil to the labourers of Great Britain, and to society, if strenuous efforts had not been made to raise the standard (still unfortunately much too low) of Irish labour, on the one hand, and, on the other, to facilitate its emigration to younger lands. What, however, we may do on our own territory we cannot do on foreign soil. We can only face the evil, if it is one, now threatened, by consideration of how to treat it when it reaches our waters. Can, then, anything be done? Is it right to do anything?

Even if it were just to blame, it would be most difficult to control, the use of this cheap labour by employers. Competition, so keen where trade is free, so essentially part of free trade, puts interference here, practically, out of court. It is certain that cheap labour will be seized on by some to undersell others; and this means that it must, if, and so long as, it is available, be commonly used where it appropriately meets requirements. It is labour, not of the factory, open to inspection, but of the garret, the solitary candle, and the midnight hours.

Nothing, probably, but sumptuary laws, for which

we are not yet prepared, can stop this. The remedy must be sought elsewhere.

I know that there is a variety of opinion as to the extent of this evil of foreign immigration; and that able statistics have been put forward to show that it is not so formidable as some suppose; that the increase is not great, and that it is, to a large extent, an increase only in transit.

I have no desire, and, indeed, no power to argue this point; but I recognise the well-known fact that a small element of underselling is strong in reducing price; and I feel bound to regard as the most authoritative view, the Report of the Select Committee of the House of Commons on the subject, in 1889, which announced as its conclusion that the evil was a growing one of serious dimensions, and that before long the wisdom of the nation would have, of necessity, to grapple with it, and find a remedy.

In writing this paper I am not putting myself forward as an advocate, strongly, of any particular remedy. I do not know enough to do so. I am not in a position to do it if I did. I am merely, at request, putting down some points for consideration on what I find suggested.

The prominent suggestion—indeed, the Select Committee itself named it as the only effectual one—is a prohibition against the importation of this cheap labour; and it calls for a great deal of reflection.

As a merely abstract point, prohibition of importation is not an unknown entity amongst us.

We prohibit various things—piratical books, false coins, indecent works of any kind, false trade marks or indications, disease in human beings, and in special shapes in animals, products dangerous to life, such as explosives, or adulterated provisions ; besides various other things touching our revenue. Prohibition, therefore, *per se*, would be no innovation. It would be new only, if adopted in this matter, in the extended purview in a fresh direction.

At present, our prohibitions may be put under the following categories :—

Protection of mere life from disease or accident ;

Protection from disease in the means of subsistence, and the adulteration of them ;

Protection from falseness in the medium of purchase of subsistence ;

Protection of public morals, and of honesty in trade.

To go beyond these in the direction suggested would be the doing of two things more : viz.—beyond mere life, the protection of our habits of life, so as to prevent their deterioration—to say not only, " You sha'n't come in to kill us," but, further, " You sha'n't come in to lower our mode of life ; " and, in doing this, to make use of the powers of the Government,

not only to prevent trade being dishonest, but to
secure its financial tone, and its scale of remuneration.

This is the change which the suggestion means, or,
at least, which it would effect as regards advance in
prohibition.

Perhaps it may be further than strict political
economy would authorize us to go. I am not sure of
this when it is a question of human beings starving
out other human beings from their natural rights.
But take it so; and yet we have it on the highest
authority that the philosophy of political economy
may be banished, with safety, to Jupiter or Saturn,
when national urgency demands its expulsion.

There are, however (and the question should be
treated with complete frankness), reasons, besides
political economy, why we should, at first, shrink
from the step of prohibition, and *that* notwithstanding
the example of other countries.

Many of these unfortunate beings are flying not
merely from poverty, but from persecution; from
death and cruelty, to the merest patch of life in peace.
The shores of England are supposed to be the free
haven for any suffering, sorrow, or distress that
chooses to seek them. It is one of our glories. We
would not willingly turn from it, though it may exist
to our own hindrance. Pity, wonder what else can
possibly become of the poor things, would restrain us

unless duty, where duty most is due, imperatively points otherwise.

Then, again, the free ingress of foreign element is, as an abstract rule, a benefit to the nations. This has always been so in the dissemination of arts and industries; and, although, at times, in the history of the world, it has led to a lessening of physical strength, it has scarcely ever failed in the increase of civilization.

"*Græcia capta ferum victorem cepit.*" The arts and culture of conquered Greece took captive the conquering, but merely physical, force of Rome by the influx of Greeks over the Roman provinces.

The circumstances of the world now render no longer dangerous to us the cultivation which emasculated the Roman; and the various immigrations which religious persecutions and other upheavals have thrown on our shores, only taught us useful and artistic improvements. They have never weakened, they have always strengthened us.

The country in Europe which has been most free to foreigners—the Netherlands—has long been marked as one of the richest and most self-reliant.

Reluctance, therefore, to exclude a foreign element is part both of our feelings, our history, and our self-interest; and the question whether we have a sufficient reason for exclusion, in this instance, is, consequently, one to be approached with great care; but I think that the consideration of it may, possibly, be helped by

a short statement of how, as regards arrival, and freedom to trade and work, and other political necessities,
our law and history has treated aliens, and treats them
now.

Some of these provisions may, in quoting, seem to be
but obsolete enactments of a system to which we have
bid farewell—a system of interfering paternal government, inconsistent with the present elevation of individual freedom. But he would be a bold man who
would affirm that the battle between individualism
and socialism has left the ring. It would be safer to
allege that the concluding "round" has yet to be
fought out, on thoroughly doubtful odds.

The extremes of such a combat raise their voices.
On one side, there are ardent politicians who would
elevate the individual to such a pedestal as not even
to tax him without his personal consent. On the
other hand, there are prophets of socialism who fore-
cast all human life controlled in every action of state,
of commerce, and of property, by rules for communal
benefit.

Who can positively say that we may not yet search,
for instructive guidance, the less individual legislation
of our ancestors? Who can tell that society may not
yet place itself, with common acceptance, in leading
strings even tighter than any which guided it in the
days at which we are now disposed to smile with
superior compassion.

Sovereign States possess the right internationally to
order aliens out of their respective territories, or to
prevent their admission therein.   It is stated that, in
our common law, there is a prerogative in this respect
vested in the Crown, as an appendant to its power of
declaring war.   But the extent of the right is doubtful, and the regulation of trading permission and
social life has been mainly exercised under, and by
virtue of, special Acts of Parliament, as the exigencies
of the country required, and as the varying views
taken of the desirability of admitting foreign traffic
and intercourse oscillated to and fro.

The dealing with aliens so far in our history has
turned mainly on two points—interference with trade,
and political agitation.   The present point—its conflict
with the labour market—is a question chiefly of this
day.   I propose to shortly recount the dealings with
the first two questions.   Possibly, thereby, judgment
may be aided as to how far it is right to deal with the
third.

In the great Charter, and the Statutes confirming
it, it was provided that :—

" All merchants, unless they were openly prohibited
before, shall have safe and sure conduct to depart out
of England, and to come into England, and to tarry in
and go through England, as well by land as by water,
to buy or sell without any evil tolls by the old and
rightful customs, except in time of war."

This was the generous pronouncement of the Charter of our liberties. It mentions merchants only, probably because merchants then, alone, travelled. Whether it would have gone beyond this, if communication had been then as now, cannot be affirmed; but, at the time, it more probably meant free access to all strangers likely to reach our shores.

And yet it was very long before, and only after various changes, that this freedom became complete as to even merchants.

During the immediately succeeding reigns of the early Plantagenet kings, it is quite clear that equality of position was denied to alien merchants; and, until the reign of Edward I., they suffered here, as in many other European countries, great disabilities, and, notably, amongst them, the unjust liability of being arrested, one of them, for the debt or crime of another.

The policy, however, of that great king, the first really English king of the Norman conquest, was to encourage foreign trade, and especially the woollen trade, in aid of agricultural England; and his Parliament enacted that, " in no city, borough, or town should any person be distrained for any debt whereof he is not debtor or pledge."

This policy was taken up, confirmed, and extended by his grandson, Edward III., whose Parliaments enacted, amongst other things :—

" That all merchant strangers may go and come

with their merchandises into England after the tenour of the Great Charter; and that all merchant aliens might buy or sell corn, wine, goods, flesh, fowl, and all other provisions and victuals, wools, cloths, ware, merchandises, and all other things, and freely pass and sell them without interruption."

It is, however, clear that these free trade views were those rather of the monarch than of the people. Edward III. was, in his personal character, his firm position, and his brilliant successes, strong enough to force his own views on even a reluctant people.

For centuries after his death, the policy of the country and its laws as to alien trade swung round in the opposite direction.

Restrictions, disabilities and practical prohibitions, dictated by the corporations of the towns and their guilds, took the place of freedom, encouragement and even privilege.

Until the strong Tudor times no Sovereign stood in Edward's independent position. Feebleness of character, doubtful claims to the succession, dynastic wars and family rivalries, alike, combined to keep the Sovereign subject to the feelings of the people, and the opposition of corporate monopolies.

Hence we find, in that interval, such restrictions as these, which we can only regard as those of England speaking its real voice at that time :—

In 1390, Richard II., "That no alien person should

I

trade without proof given that he would expend half
the value of his merchandise in other merchandise
here."

In 1392, after stating that the Acts of Edward
III. were a great hindrance and damage to cities of the
realm, that " no foreign merchant should sell or buy
within the realm to any other foreign merchant to sell
again; that no foreign merchant should sell at retail
within the realm except provisions, and as to some
provisions, only in large quantities," thus forbidding
retail trade to foreigners almost altogether; and forbidding wholesale traffic except with British subjects.

This was followed, in 1402, Henry IV., by provisions forbidding any carrying of the proceeds of
such trade out of the country, except in the shape of
other merchandise bought in exchange.

This was a great retrogression, from the full freedom of the Charter, and the Edwards, to restriction of
manner of trade, and restriction as to export.

But two stronger measures followed.

In 1429, Henry VI., there was an enactment, somewhat interesting in these days of contest between
mono-metallism and bi-metallism. Despite prohibition, the aliens evidently managed to take away coin
with them. Both standards obtained then, and for
many years afterwards; but, with a shrewd eye for
business, the traders were in the habit of refusing

silver, which won no premium in their own countries, and requiring, in payment, only gold, which did.

This refusal was emphatically declared illegal in 1429, and the law then passed is a strong instance of that species of paternal government rendering "contracts out of an act" illegal, of which we see specimens in the present day. It provides that:—

"No merchant alien shall constrain or bind any of the King's liege people by promise, covenant, or bond, to make payment to him in gold for any manner of debt "—and, further, "To prevent the great loss which persons of this realm have by losses made of their merchandises to merchant aliens, no Englishman shall sell within this realm, or cause to be sold to any merchant alien, any manner of merchandise for any but ready payment in money, or else in merchandise, to be paid and counted in hand on pain of forfeiture of the same." [1]

The exclusion of pauper aliens may be a strong measure, but it would be a trifle compared to this inquisitorial Act in the reign of England's feeblest king, forbidding, paternally, any trust of any kind to an alien in this country. We should certainly be astonished at an Act telling us, now, whom we may give credit to, and whom not. And, yet, are we so very far from it

---

[1] This was extended to a permission of six months' credit by an early subsequent Act.

in these days of Jupiter and Saturn, of tenants who may only agree on statutory terms, and of artisans who ask to be prevented by law from selling their capital, the labour of their hands, as each may think right ?

Then, there was another enactment which tells even more on the immediate point—a law regulating the location of aliens while trading in this country.

By an Act in 1439 (Henry VI.), not repealed until this century, it was enacted :—

"That all alien merchants shall be under the survey of certain persons, to be called Hosts or Surveyors, to be appointed by the Mayors of the several cities and to be good and credible natives, expert in merchandise." "Such Hosts to be privy to all sales and contracts of the Alien." "Aliens to sell all their merchandise within eight months on pain of forfeiture." "The Hosts to keep books in which to register all contracts, etc., of aliens, and deliver a transcript thereof to the Exchequer." "The Hosts to have 2*d*. in the £ on all such contracts," "and to be sworn to be faithful," and "any alien refusing to submit to these regulations to be imprisoned until security given to comply with them."

Restrictions on trade led naturally to restrictions on manufacture.

In 1483, in the reign of Richard III., it was enacted :—

"That no person not born under the King's obey-

sance shall exercise or occupy any handicraft, or the
occupation of any handicraftsman in this realm of
England, but that all such persons shall (after date
then fixed) depart into their own country again, or
else be servants to such of the King's subjects only as
be expert and cunning in such Feats, Wits, and Crafts
which the said strangers can occupy." [1]

In the reign of King Henry VII. (1491), when the
death of James III. of Scotland had strained the relations between the two Kingdoms, an Act was passed
simply in these words:—"All Scots not made Denizens
shall depart this Realm within forty days after proclamation upon pain of forfeiture of all their goods."
While, one step further, in the reign of Queen Mary,
there is a Statute, directed against the French, in time
of difference with that nation, which, also, boldly
directed their departure from the realm and based it,
by the preamble, not only on political grounds, but
because the influx of such strangers tended to the
diminishing of the subjects of the Realm and the
treasure of the Sovereign.

Such, in very brief instances, was the policy of the
late Plantagenet and the early Tudor reigns. I do
not suggest that it was a treatment more harsh than
that of other countries. It was accompanied by

---

[1] This, by several Statutes, and, notably, by one of Henry
VII., was not to apply to subjects of the Hanse Towns.

various enactments against the ill usage or illegal over-charging of aliens; and although, in some respects, the alien was charged more than the subject, in other respects he was charged less; and his own wit led him to evade much that told against him.

But any allegation that our history has always opened our shores to all trade and advent of aliens without restriction, is incorrect as to this period. The feeling of the people was otherwise; and the Sovereigns and Parliament followed it in their policy of action.

There are, probably, few things in the history of the world which have so completely failed in their object as religious persecution amongst Christians in the last few centuries. It reduced Spain, where it had its way, from a great empire to a third-rate power. It led France to revolution and free-thought. It raised Holland from enslavement as a Catholic Province to a great free Protestant community. While, above all things, it not only fixed England as an outwork against itself, which no storms have shaken, but it changed the policy of that country on the point under consideration.

A Protestant Queen of England, with a firm hand to repress real danger, brave, vigorous and patriotic, could afford to think, and had to think of persecution elsewhere. A Protestant alien in Europe began to look to Queen Elizabeth of England as his guardian.

Even the trade prejudices of the country yielded before this sympathetic demand.

In the reign of the great Queen, the alien laws began silently, and without objection, to be unenforced, and the persecution of Alva in the Netherlands, sent to his master's greatest enemy a number of useful and law-abiding subjects, filled with the knowledge of arts and sciences, and calculated to be a wholesome leaven to a still stronger and more agricultural people.[1]

The Acts of the Plantagenets and early Tudors grew into desuetude ; and, in the reign of Charles II., after the storms of domestic discord, it was enacted that aliens might legally trade and manufacture in all the leading industries of the nation.

This was two years before the revocation of the Edict of Nantes, and it was a fitting prelude to that memorable event.

The prejudices of the nation, and its corporate exclusiveness gave way to the brotherhood of religion; and, in the reign of Queen Ann, in 1708, there was passed the Act for the Naturalization of Foreign Protestants, which is the foundation of our present laws for the easy naturalization of foreigners.

During the first eighty years of the Guelphic

---

[1] Queen Elizabeth, however, made no scruple as to the handling of aliens where her feelings led her. By simple Proclamation she ordered expulsion of Scots.

dynasty, and despite pretensions to the Throne, no special Alien Act appears to have been contemplated. But, with the great upheaval of foreign thought and foreign Government which convulsed the end of the last century, a new consideration of the question of aliens came upon this country, namely, that of deep political and moral danger.

The provisions as to aliens in the Georgian and Victorian eras are of three kinds, which may be classified as follows :—

(*a*) War Alien Acts.

(*b*) Peace Alien Acts.

(*c*) Registration Acts—these last of two degrees of stringency.

The Alien Acts contain regulations (varying between peace time and war time) for expulsion of aliens if the State requires it. In all of them power of expulsion is conferred on the central authority. In war time it is more stringent. All these Acts contain also provisions as to registration.

The chronological history of these Acts, put briefly, is as follows :—

In 1793, in the throes of the French Revolution, there was the first Alien Act, which, being of a stringent character, became the model " War Alien Act." This continued, with amendments, until the Peace of Amiens, in 1802. Then, for a year, there was a Peace Alien Act, followed, in the succeeding year, by a War Alien Act, when the Peninsular War began. With the first French Restoration there was in 1814, a Peace Alien Act, followed again, in the year ensuing, by a War Alien Act, with the temporary restoration of the French Empire; and, again, by a Peace Alien Act, when the power of Napoleon was finally crushed.

This last statute was renewed, by biennial continuance Acts, until, in 1826, the expulsion clauses were entirely removed, and registration only remained.

This registration was modified by the Act of 6 and 7 William IV. c. 11 (1836), the present Alien Act, and the only disturbance of its free and generous treatment has been the temporary Chartist Act of 1848, 11 & 12 of the Queen c. 20, which was an Expulsion Act, passed for one year.

This is the oscillating history of these Acts, growing from that first passed in 1793.

Describing them generally, their force was this :—

In the war times, aliens were liable to expulsion at the entire discretion of the Government, and also to various other restrictions as to movements in the country and otherwise. In peace, to expulsion only on more special grounds.

Before 1836, registration was required to be made by the alien himself on landing, and also, at stated intervals, afterwards to an "Alien Office." By the Act of that year, registration, so far as the alien him-

self was concerned, was limited to a landing statement
to be rendered to the customs officer. That absolved
the alien; all the rest was official. And this is the
law that at present stands in the statute book.

It will thus be seen that the great epochs as to
alien expulsion in the last hundred years were :—

The Reign of Terror; the outbreak of war after the
Peace of Amiens; the Hundred Days' Reign; and
the Chartist and Revolutionary Upheaval of 1848.

The Restriction Acts of these epochs did not, however, as is well known, pass into law without strong
opposition ; and the debates which accompanied them
are not the least memorable in our history, either in
forensic ability or dramatic effect.

The Bills were introduced by Governments of
varying party politics. The first was moved by Mr.
Pitt's Government, supported by Mr. Burke, and
opposed by Mr. Fox. That in 1816 was moved by
Lord Castlereagh, and opposed by Lord (then Mr.)
Brougham. That in 1848 was introduced by the
Government of Lord (then Lord John) Russell, and
opposed by Sir William Molesworth, Mr. Joseph
Hume, and Mr. Bright.

Both great parties of the State, when in office,
deemed such Acts necessary, and carried them by
large majorities. For right or for wrong, such was
the fact.

No doubt great impulses at those epochs swayed

the country. It was in supporting the Bill of 1793 that Mr. Burke, in a speech of impassioned oratory, denouncing "the French murderers and atheists," and urging the absolute necessity of keeping them out of these realms, drew from his breast the dagger which he had kept concealed there, and "in frenzied declamation" threw it on the floor of the House. "I warn my countrymen," he said, "to beware of these execrable philosophers": "*hic niger est, hunc tu Romane caveto.*"

The oratory of statesmen, however, on one side or the other, is not so sure a guide as the calm study of history, and the dry legislative results which indicate rightly enough, in the main, the wish and policy of the nation.

The vigorous statements in opposition—

> In 1793, that "the proposed measure was in direct violation of the law and the Constitution," and "would be an illegal suspension of the laws of the land."

> In 1815 and 1816, that "to the Constitution such a measure was unknown, as the Constitution allowed free ingress and egress to all foreigners without restriction;" that "it was an innovation upon the laws of the land and the principles of the Constitution."

are not borne out by the legislative history of the Plantagenet and early Tudor reigns.

Nor that, in 1848, that "it had been the privilege of England in all times to afford unrestricted hospitality to the unfortunates of all countries in the world, and that not only by law, but from the natural inclination of the national mind and character."

History rather justifies the words of Sir George Grey, in introducing the Bill: "The grounds on which it is proposed are simply those which this country has always maintained, and has every right to maintain, namely, that of self-protection."[1]

The Act of 1848 soon expired. An Act for a similar purpose now, when the naturalization of foreigners is so easy, would have to be either prohibitory of admission, or to extend to naturalized subjects.

The Registration Act of 6 & 7 William IV. c. 36 is now, therefore, the last Act standing on the Statute Book on this subject, and it is the one generally spoken of now as "the Alien Act."

---

[1] In all these debates considerable discussion took place as to the meaning of the words in the Great Charter, "unless they were openly prohibited before" (*nisi antea publicè prohibiti*). Did this reserve a royal prerogative, or only a statutory power? or what, if anything precise, did it point to? So far, however, as aliens themselves are concerned it is of little moment to them by what special branch of the governmental machinery the law adverse to them becomes law. The point is only interesting as indicating how far and in what direction expulsion was in the constitution, somewhere, a reserved right.

It provides, in section 2, for a report by the master of every arriving ship, showing the number of aliens on board or landed, with penalties for non-compliance. In section 3 for a declaration by the aliens themselves of their names and country and other particulars. In sections 4 and 5, for registration of these declarations, and transmission of a copy to the Secretary of State.

For the first of these requirements special provision is made in the form of ship's "Report" prescribed by the Customs Acts, which has a heading, "Number of Alien Passengers, if any." But the enactment generally has, of late years, and probably with intent and from feelings of confidence, been but loosely observed. The crudescence of the present question, and the desire expressed for more accurate statistics, have led to a more strict revival of section 1 in the ports especially affected. At the ports of rapid channel transit close observance is not attainable; but those ports are not the inlets of destitute poverty.

In brief sketch this is the history of our law and statutes as to aliens. It shows a great leaning on the part of our country to generous hospitality. From the Great Charter downwards this has never been wholly forgotten, even in the hardest and most selfish times.

On the other hand, it is impossible to affirm, with truth, that it has ever been the fixed policy of our country to hold itself bound to this view against proved national interests.

Taking the statutory history from first to last, and giving it close study, the conclusion it leads to is rather that, while hospitality, free and unfettered, is loved and wished for, if it can be properly conceded, national interests are, and ever have been in the history of our country, deemed the superior call.

Is there, then, this superior call in the present subject-matter? Does an influx which, unassimilating as it is, threatens a progressive lowering of wage-earning in our working-classes, constitute such a call?

The evil is in our lowest class. That is true. But the lowest class can least defend themselves; and the lowest price, moreover, rules the higher markets.

Previous legislation rested on exceptional circumstances, and found opposed acceptance only on that ground. Is the present an exceptional circumstance as serious as political and moral danger?

Views on this may differ; but, compared with the position under which the previous legislation obtained, the circumstances are certainly, in one sense, utterly exceptional.

Rapid communication which, in these days, has changed the world, force on us new and exceptional views.

The evolutions of science may evolve a new political

economy, and establish, by their own force, accepted by the rest of the world, a superior call, where, in our spirit and our sentiment, we should, in the abstract, least desire it.

But, grant it to be a superior call, then comes the last question, Is it practicable for us to do it? A call, however imperative, is limited by practicability.

Some of our colonies and various other countries have adopted plans of prohibition—notably the legislation of the United States. No aliens are admitted there without proof of some standing, and some means of supporting themselves without detriment to the community. Without this proof they are sent back as " returned empties."

It does not, however, necessarily follow that such steps can be adopted here. There is no traditional history to tie the hands of these younger countries. Their examples are not necessarily appropriate to these isles of ours, where trade is freer and inspection less close. Our country is the centre and depôt of the world's trade and intercourse; while transit to our nearest ports is over a very small silvery streak.

We have therefore in this, as in other things, our special difficulties to face. But I am sufficiently optimistic to believe that if our country once decided that this was an evil which must be met, the precise method of facing it would work itself out, as most things do with us.

If we arrive at the conclusion of the old Greek chorus, ψηφίζομεν τὶ δρᾶν, "we are decided that something must be done," I feel it impossible to doubt that the wisdom of our administrators would find some means, not inconsistent with our history and our policy, to check an evil to the community at large, and to our great centres of population especially.

> "London, the needy villains' general home;
> The common sewer of Paris and of Rome,
> Condemned by fortune and resistless fate,
> Sucks in the dregs of each corrupted State."

Such are the words which, in one of the great alien debates in 1848, were quoted as to our vast metropolis. Vast it was then; it is now—it seems almost fabulous to state it—twice as vast. It has sprung from two and a half to nearly five millions in those four decades. It has advanced also in beauty, in enlarged thoroughfares, in magnificent streets, in grand open spaces, in great sanitary works, in multiplied opportunities of health, and enjoyment for the masses. Are we to say that in the extrinsic debasement of its lowest class we are powerless to mend it?

Queen Elizabeth, in 1593, thought that London had grown large enough for the proper management of any congregation of human beings. In that year she passed an Act which, reciting that London "doth daily grow and increase by reason of the pestering of

houses with divers families, and the harbouring of
inmates, whereby great infection of sickness and
dearth of victuals and fuel hath grown and increased,"
enacted that "no person or persons should from
thenceforth make or erect any new building or build-
ings, house or houses for habitation or dwelling,
within three miles of the gates of the city." London
contained then only 150,000 inhabitants—not very
much more than its now annual increase.

This remarkable Act remained on our Statute Book
until its repeal only three years ago. It is almost to
be regretted that it has disappeared, and that so
curious an historical fossil has been thus obliterated.
Moreover, although it has not, as events have shown,
been strictly observed! it was not without its effect
on the shape of the growth and the configuration of
London; nor is the interest of it altogether past.

The dangers then apprehended were, in their precise form, met bravely, boldly grappled with, and
surmounted; and we can justly afford to smile at
some of the fears and the views of those days.

And yet the underlying current of them is with us
still. It is still London which "sucks in the dregs of
each corrupted State;" still there is amongst us "the
pestering of houses with divers families," and thereby
the "infection of sickness and the dearth of victuals
and fuel," as in the days of the great Tudor Queen.

Are we to touch this disease in its most feverish

development? And if so, how far and in what way
is it wise? how far and in what way is it right,
national, just, and benevolent, that we should touch
it in these more experienced days of a still greater
Queen? That is the question!

THE IMPERIAL ASPECT.

By W. A. McArthur.

The average Englishman is very proud of his empire—
perhaps, at times, even a little arrogant. He is never
tired of telling the world how the sun never sets on
his flag. He is always declaring his cheerful willing-
ness to die for the empire at a moment's notice. He
loves the poems which talk of the flag which has
braved the storms of every sea, and which never floats
over a slave. The unity of the empire has been a
most successful electioneering cry. A new society
has sprung into being, under most distinguished
patronage, to forward the movement for the federation
of the empire. Everybody joins it. Speakers find in
the empire matter for glowing perorations—it is a
safe subject for a leading article. Even among the
politicians in the House of Commons, who have long
since lost belief in most things, there may be found
some who still hold to their faith in the empire.

All this indeed is to the good. No one who has
seen with an intelligent eye the countries which make
up the British Empire, can fail to return to England
stirred to the very soul with a sense of the enormous

possibilities which lie before these vast territories, which the courage and enterprise of Englishmen have added to their empire. And no impartial observer can fail to see that on the whole the empire of England is a factor in the world which makes for righteousness. Wherever our flag is planted there follow the arts of peace. And there follows also the spirit of fair play and of just dealings with native races which has made our government always tolerated, and in most cases welcomed by peoples the most diverse in race and religion and character.

All this is true, and it is well that the original John Bull at home should appreciate it, and be proud of it, and be always ready to cheer for his empire. But his testing time has yet to come. Up to the present he has had nothing to do for his empire but to cheer and to pay the bill. And this, to do him justice, he has always done cheerfully enough. But the world moves fast, and in matters of opinion it moves faster in the English world outside England than it does in England itself. And John Bull will find out that, if he is to realize his dream of a federation of the empire, he must do more than cheer for his colonies and pay some of their bills. It is good that he should cheer, and also, within limits, that he should pay. But he must also do violence to some of his opinions. He must give up some of his pet prejudices. He must be content to sink, to some extent, his own individuality. He can no longer pose as the all-powerful father. He must take his place as the wise elder brother of the English family. And he must admit that there are some things which his younger brothers can teach even him, and in which their experience may be a useful guide to him.

This is a hard saying for John Bull. No one, on the whole, has such useful prejudices as the good John. And he has found many of them serve him so well in the past that he clings to them with a dogged desperation which has become almost a part of his religion. We lay violent hands on the very Ark of the Covenant when we assail John Bull on any of these dear beliefs of his. And yet, if we are to make any progress with the subject of which this book treats, we shall have to attack John Bull on two of his most cherished illusions.

He believes in Free Trade as he does in the Thirty-nine Articles. He probably does not quite understand either, but he is convinced they are necessary for salvation. Protection he will not have in any shape. And for England itself no doubt he is right. Probably, also, for most of her colonies, though many of them have taken a different view, being under different conditions. But his belief in Free Trade, like all the beliefs he holds strongly, becomes to him a sort of fetish. He has blindly worshipped it so long and so ardently that, like Mr. Dick, who found it impossible to keep the head of Charles I. out of his memoirs, our good John finds an attack on Free Trade in every proposal for legislative interference with anybody or anything which comes into this country. He jumps to the conclusion that we are tampering with his most cherished principles in trying to exclude the pauper foreigner. But if he would learn from one of the most flourishing of his colonies, that of New South Wales, which is a free trade colony, he would find that she has long ago, despite her almost pedantic devotion to free trade, taken very strong steps indeed to shut out such immigrants from other countries as have seemed to her undesirable. I am not now referring to the Chinese. They are practically excluded from Australia also, though for a different reason, and I will return to their case later on. But I am referring now to instances in which Australia has refused to admit English subjects, natives of these islands, for reasons that have seemed to her to be sufficient. And, indeed, so strong has been her determination to keep her people free from moral contamination, that she has at times refused admission to English-born subjects even without the authority of a law to back her. When the Irish informers, after the trial of the Phœnix Park murderers, attempted to land in Australia, neither New South Wales nor Victoria would receive them. Their action was grossly illegal. It had no legal sanction. And yet the Home

Government had no choice but to acquiesce in the decision of the Colonial Government, it being felt to be an impossible thing to attempt to coerce a great colony into receiving scoundrels of this class.

Most of the colonies have also taken steps to prevent the introduction of persons likely to become a charge upon the public or upon charitable institutions. And in so doing they have only followed the general practice of the world outside the British Isles. The whole weight of colonial opinion and experience is in the direction of imposing reasonable restrictions on the introduction of undesirable elements into their society. They acted in the case of the Irish informers upon moral grounds. They are acting in the case of the Chinese upon material as well as moral grounds. The Chinaman has about as low a standard of comfort as can be imagined. It is a standard which apparently cannot be raised to our level; at all events, not in Australia. And therefore they have been practically excluded from these colonies, in absolute defiance of treaties between England and China. I should like to see the English Colonial Secretary who would at this time of day attempt to interfere with the Anti-Chinese legislation of Australia. Sir Henry Parkes, the premier of New South Wales, when charged with having broken the laws of the land in excluding the Chinese, replied, " I care nothing about your cobweb of technical law; I am obeying a law far superior

to any law which issued these permits, namely, the
law of the preservation of society in New South
Wales." That this is the right attitude no one who
knows the habits of the Chinese can doubt. It is, of
course, an attitude which shocks the pedantic free
trader. It is an attitude which is not for the benefit
of the consumer. If the be-all and end-all of government is to obtain unrestricted competition at the price
of public morality and of decency of life, then no
doubt Australia is wrong. But if it be a good thing
to risk paying a shade more for a nation's goods, in
order to exclude a moral plague which may turn a
great city into a modern Sodom, then there is no
friend of his kind who will not approve Sir Henry
Parkes' declaration, and the action of the New South
Wales and other Australian governments. I am justified in saying that the Imperial view—that is the view
of almost the whole of the empire outside of England—
is in favour of the restrictions we are seeking to obtain
in England. Is it not a strong thing for England
absolutely to refuse to listen to the teachings of the
experience of almost every English-speaking community in the world except herself?

And how, in face of her persistent defiance of
English opinion outside England, can she hope to
succeed with her pet project of Imperial Federation?
There can be no such federation without some kind
of mutual give and take. Indeed, on this point of

Chinese immigration, Mr. Gillies, the then premier
of Victoria, declared that he was not aware of the
exact nature and extent of the obligations of the Imperial Government to China; and went on to argue
that as the colonies had had no voice in the making
of these treaties their governments could not be held
to be bound to receive Chinese immigration to an
indefinite extent. This is one of the points, and a
most important point too, upon which John Bull must
be content to sink his prejudices and learn from his
younger brothers before he can convince them of the
benefit of a closer union with him.

This Australian determination to preserve themselves from moral contamination is no new thing; nor
has it sprung into being over the recent dispute about
Chinese immigration. The feeling on that subject, as
I have already shown, is so strong in Australia, that
the Chinese are now practically excluded from Australia in absolute defiance of the treaties made
between England and China, which give citizens of
the Chinese Empire the right to go to Australia, or to
any other part of the British Empire, if they please.
The same restriction is applied to Chinamen who are
actually English subjects, and colonial feeling is so
strong upon this point, and so general throughout all
classes of the community, that, illegal as it may be—
in total disregard of treaty-rights as it is—no English
government has yet been found courageous enough to

disregard what is practically a unanimous colonial opinion.

I venture to prophesy that we shall never witness the intervention of the Imperial government in order to compel English subjects in Australia to carry out the treaty-rights which England has provided for the Chinese, or that such intervention will ever be used to compel Australia to receive Chinese immigrants who may even be actually British subjects.

I said just now that the Australian action against undesirable immigration was no new thing !

Between 1840 and 1850 Victoria was prepared to prevent, by force if necessary, the landing of British convicts at Melbourne. They passed in 1852 the "Convicts Prevention Act," which prevented convicts who were pardoned, or whose time had expired, or who had received tickets-of-leave, authorising them to go where they pleased in Australia, from landing in Victoria; and which imposed heavy fines upon the captains of ships attempting to introduce such passengers.

I do not think that in Australia these laws are dictated by any race-hatred, or by any religious prejudice.

There is no desire, so far as I have ever experienced, to shut out Chinese *qua* Chinese—or to shut out any other kind of immigrant solely because it may be thought that he is likely to add to the compe-

tition which prevails already in the colonial labour
market—or because he is of a different religion to the
bulk of the community. Australian opinion usually
puts the case against Chinese, against ex-convicts,
and against undesirable immigration generally, upon
high moral grounds—upon the grounds that the Aus-
tralians have a new country, with an educated, intelligent, and moral population, and that they are not
willing to run the chance of seeing that population
corrupted by the introduction of a horde of immigrants, whose habits of life, whose notions of morality,
and whose standard of comfort, are far below that of
the existing population.

Nor is the agitation against the Chinese connected
with any movement in favour of protection.

Sir Henry Parkes, whose words I have already
quoted, is premier of a free-trade cabinet in the free-
trade colony of New South Wales. The Hon. Mr. Mc
Millan is his colonial treasurer—also a very strong
free-trader, and one of the most prominent leaders in
the recent struggle between free-traders and protec-
tionists in New South Wales. He says to the electors
of East Sydney, "We have decided, although perhaps in a precipitate manner, that our virgin soil
shall not be contaminated by hordes of an alien and
unmixable race."

In one of his speeches upon this subject, Sir Henry
Parkes takes up the very strong ground that the un-

restricted introduction of Chinese into Australia would absolutely change the whole character of the Australian people.

Abandoning for a moment the argument on the ground of public morality, he declares that "they are a superior set of people belonging to a nation of an old and deep-rooted civilization. We know the beautiful results of many of their handicraft; we know how wonderful are their powers of imagination, their endurance, and their patient labour. It is for these qualities that I do not want them to come here. The influx of a few million of Chinese here would entirely change the character of this young Australian commonwealth. It is, then, because I believe the Chinese to be a powerful race, capable of taking a great hold upon the country, and because I wish to preserve the type of my own nation in these fair countries, that I am, and always have been, opposed to the influx of Chinese."

Now I am not arguing here in favour of race-antipathies, or of religious hatred; and I am far from advocating that anybody should break the law. I am only using the Australian example, which shows their feeling to be so strong that they have even risked the defiance of treaty-rights, and the breaking of English law, in order to keep out what they regard as being undesirable immigrants, and in order to preserve the type of their own race, to prove how strong is colonial

opinion upon these points, and how vitally necessary
for the welfare of their country they believe to be the
powers which they have taken for the exclusion of
such people from their shores.

Is it not, then, a strange thing for England to
refuse to learn lessons which are the result of the
experience of every other English-speaking nation in
the world ? For it must not be forgotten that the
United States also have found the burden of undesirable immigrants intolerable. Twenty years ago
America was inclined to be proud of the number of
her immigrants, but within, comparatively speaking,
the last few years, they have begun to pour in upon
her in swarms from all parts of Europe, until she has
become saturated, so to say, with very much the same
class of immigrant whom we are seeking to exclude
from England.

These immigrants—many of them—do not speak
English, and do not assimilate with the population as
do immigrants of the Scandinavian, German, and
even Irish type. They bring with them a low
standard of morals, and a low standard of physical
comfort, and they therefore compete unfairly with
existing labour in America, which has, for the most
part, attained the enjoyment of a wage which enables
it to live in tolerable comfort. There serious troubles
have recently arisen from this very cause. They find
that the lower class of foreign immigrants have secret

societies of their own, with objects which are not
compatible with the obligations of respectable citizenship. Some of these evils have recently come to light
in the most marked manner during the Mafia Riots in
New Orleans; and although the lynching of the
Italians in New Orleans, whom the American citizens
regarded as having been acquitted, owing to the
terrorising or bribing of the jury by a secret Italian
murder society, was no doubt grossly illegal, and
ought to be repudiated in the name of law and order,
yet there is not the slightest doubt that the entire
current of American unofficial opinion is very strongly
with the citizens of New Orleans, who are regarded as
having on the whole taken the only course open to
them to free themselves from the burden of an intolerable foreign tyranny. The presentment of the grand
jury of New Orleans points out that there is no question more intimately connected with the subject
matter of their investigation than immigration, and
records its opinion " that the time has past when this
country (America) can be made the dumping-ground
for the worthless and depraved of every nation."

Amongst the foreign miners in America there is
also a grievous trouble. The Russian and Italian
miners are in open and armed revolt against the law,
and so strong is the public opinion which has been
stirred up in the face of all these facts, that it is very
probable indeed that the United States will pass

legislation excluding from their country all immigrants—pauper or otherwise—excepting English, German, Scandinavian, and perhaps the Swiss.

In the face of all the experience of other English-speaking races it seems to me impossible that England can stand still. America has an area of some three million square miles with a population of between sixty and seventy millions. Australia has about the same area of country with a population of between four and five millions. If these young countries, with a practically boundless supply of land, and so comparatively sparse a population, find it expedient to exclude the pauper foreigner—nay, more, regard it as so vital to their interests to do so that they are willing to run the risk of European complication in the one case, and of infringing treaty rights and breaking the law in the other, in order to accomplish their object—how much the more necessary is it for us? We possess in England one hundred and twenty thousand square miles, as against three million, with a population of, say, thirty millions of souls. Neither America nor Australia, with an infinitely smaller ratio of inhabitants to their acreage, can afford to allow free entry to all comers. Nor, I think, can we. It is surely time that our old country should wake out of her sleep and set herself resolutely to work to purge herself of her dangerous foreign elements while there is yet time.

The other argument which sorely oppresses John Bull is the argument in connection with political refugees. He fears that if legislation of this kind be passed, he may be found some day handing over continental political prisoners to the tender mercies of despotic governments. It is a fear which does him credit, but which, I think, is not well founded. Means might very well be devised to shield the political refugee. To begin with, very few of them come here as paupers, and still fewer come who are totally unknown, and whose cases could not therefore be enquired into before they were sent back.

Finally, I think John Bull should reflect that he owes a duty to his children. We believe the Anglo-Saxon race to be the finest of the world. Every Englishman, at home or abroad, or in America, is proud of his race, of his language, of his traditions, and of the great Anglo-Saxon stock from which he sprung. Kingsley has told us the touching story of the old warrior Wulf, who, on the point of submitting himself to Christian baptism, suddenly bethought him to inquire from the officiating bishop where were the souls of his heathen ancestors. " In hell!" replied the bishop. And Wulf drew back from the font. " He would prefer, if Adolf had no objection, to go to his own people."

So, I think, say we all. We prefer our own people and our own race. Let us see to it that we preserve

its vigour and its noble characteristics, so that our
colonial offspring may still bear themselves proudly
when they think of the parent race from which they
came. Let us be wise while yet there is time, lest in
years to come our children should despise us. Surely
they must despise us if they see us heedless alike of
our own race traditions and of the experience with
which they themselves have furnished us.

THE ITALIAN ASPECT.

By W. H. Wilkins.

ITALY, one of Nature's gardens, a land teeming with relics of the mighty past, rich in treasures of literature and art, a country great in natural resources with some of the very best staple products, is yet one of the worst as regards her economic condition. Her exports are varied and rich; but over-populated, and with an internal system which does not provide to keep her poor employed, her surplus population drifts from home to work, to beg, or to starve in other lands.

For many years the influx of Italians into this country has been very large and increasing. Italy would seem to show a partiality for England over all other countries, except perhaps America, in sending to its shores her illiterate masses. London, and many of our large provincial cities, are crowded with a class of Italians, who are, for the most part, non-producers. Abhorring agriculture, and in fact any settled occupation or trade, they cling to our large centres of population, and eke out an existence by means of the most degrading pursuits. There are, of course, notable

exceptions. I do not include in this category that
numerous class of Italians who, upon their arrival in
England, take up some definite trade or employment,
such as confectioners, cooks, and waiters. These are
in no sense an evil, for they supply a felt want. They
come to us as skilled workmen, and are decent and
cleanly in their habits and mode of life. Gradually
they are absorbed into our national life, and become
good and useful members of the community.

Unfortunately, the great mass of Italian emigrants
differ widely from such as these. They are, for the
most part, the idle, the vicious, and the destitute, the
off-scouring of their own country, who, forbidden or
hampered by the drastic laws now enforced in Italy
against vagrancy and mendicancy, drift over to
England, and here endeavour to pursue that nefarious
mode of life which is denied them in the land of their
birth.

Many Italians arrive in this country in an absolutely
destitute condition, knowing no trade and having
neither friends nor money. They apply for relief at
once, and very often upon arrival go straight from the
railway station to the Italian Consulate, and beg for
alms. They are ignorant of the country, of its language, of its laws, and being thus unamenable to any
good influences which may exist, they quickly fall into
bad hands. It is one more illustration of the truth of
Dr. Watts' old maxim, that mischief is always found

" for idle hands to do." Professional beggars lay in
wait for them, and teach them how to approach with
success the different charitable societies, or, worse still,
they fall an easy prey to one of the secret socialistic
or revolutionary leagues which abound in the metropolis. I am informed upon trustworthy authority that
the number of foreign revolutionists in this country
has very largely increased during the last three years,
and with the object-lesson which the *Mafia* in New
Orleans has recently presented to us, there can be no
doubt that in this rapid increase of foreign revolutionary societies lurk the elements of a very grave and
serious social danger. As an instance of this, the
Italian Benevolent Society quite recently befriended an
Italian on his arrival here, by providing him with the
implements of his occupation, that of a cook in a re-
staurant. He was discharged from his situation after
repeated trials, because of his dirty, filthy habits, and
because he absolutely refused to work. When without employment, he fell in with some gang of foreign
socialists, whose evil influence quickly counteracted
all the good the Benevolent Society had attempted to
do for him. He would do anything rather than work,
and came again and again to the Society, begging for
alms. At length he became such a nuisance, and was
so insolent, demanding as a right that to which he had
no right at all, that he had to be forcibly ejected from
the offices of the Society. Another case is that of a

man who has been twice sent back to Italy at the
Society's expense, and each time has found his way
back again to London. One more very recent instance
will suffice. As I am indebted for this to Signor
Reghetti, the secretary of the Italian Benevolent
Society, I will give it in his own words. He writes
in a letter dated from the Italian Consulate, April
27th, 1891 :—

"On Friday last, a man arrived by steamer from
Genoa, with the avowed purpose of begging. He had
fifty *francs* at Genoa, which he paid for his passage,
and from the dock he came at once to the Consulate,
perfectly penniless. He asked for help, and how to
get a license to go out begging on account of being
deprived of four fingers off one hand! Similar cases
often occur."

The Italians, of whom these three cases are fair
specimens, mostly come from Naples and the vicinity,
where they live in pauperism, filth and vice, with no
higher ambition than to get cheap food enough to
keep them alive. Uneducated and slovenly when they
come, they never improve, and despite all efforts to
restrain them, they persist in following here the same
mode of living which they practised at home. They
are incradicably bad, and only the fear of the law's
punishment, of which they have a lively dread, keeps
them in any way disciplined. The degraded habits of
this class of immigrants, innate and lasting as they are,

stamp them as a most undesirable set, whose affiliation with our own people must in time work great injury.

One of the most serious aspects of this question of the immigration of the destitute, and by far the saddest and most pathetic, is that which relates to the disgraceful traffic in Italian children carried on under the auspices of the *Padroni.* The employment of a large number of Italian children in England as vagrants and itinerant musicians, is a matter which has for a long time exercised the minds of philanthropic persons ; but few, save those who have made this question an especial study, have any conception of its increase and extent.

The traffic is carried on in this wise : —The children are brought over from their native country by men who obtain them from their parents for a very small sum, for a few ducats annually – a ducat equals 3s. 6d.—and upon undertaking to clothe and to feed them. The heartless parents who thus dispose of their offspring are, for the most part, very poor peasants living in Calabria and the South of Italy ; Caserta, in the South of Italy, is one of the principal places from which these vagrant children come. The land around Caserta is very poor, yielding scarcely sufficient sustenance to keep the people who dwell upon it alive, and the conditions of existence are necessarily hard in the extreme. This, perhaps, accounts to some extent for the unnatural alacrity which these parents

show in parting with their children. Their desire to
get rid of parental responsibility is no doubt stimu-
lated by the glowing tale of England's fabled wealth
which the *padrone* unfolds to them, and by the way
in which he dwells upon the rich and prosperous
future which is open to the children. Has he not
himself been once as they are? Is he not now rich,
as rich as the village usurer or the *sindaco*? So
drugging their consciences to sleep—if, indeed, they
can be said to have any conscience at all—the parents
surrender their children, and a few coins change
hands. The children are sold into what is a veritable
slavery without any heed being taken of their future,
and the parents are glad to be relieved of the present
responsibility by their maintenance and education.
It is not always the *padroni* though, who bring the
children to England. Sometimes they are consigned
to relatives, and sometimes the parents bring them
themselves; but whether they come under the care
of the parents, or the care of the *padroni*, the evil
effects of the system remain the same.

The *padroni*, that is the masters, having thus
obtained possession of the children, they bring them
by circuitous routes to England. How these slave-
drivers—for they are little better—manage to evade
the new Italian law against their traffic it is not easy
to say; but when they have once got clear of the
frontier, their course is plain. Some travel by rail-

way; but many of them actually journey on foot, from town to town, and village to village, all the way up to Dieppe or Calais, from thence crossing over to our shores.

Once arrived in England, these poor children are compelled to begin their sad career of degradation, vagrancy and hardships. They are, in fact, imported simply for the purpose of following one or the other of the vagrant professions in the streets of London, and throughout the country. We are all familiar with the little dark-eyed southerner who plays with such pathetic patience upon his wheezy accordion, and thanks us for our pence in a broken tongue. Early in the morning they are sent out with an accordion, concertina, or other instrument, and told to sing or play before houses, and there to wait for money. As a rule, they do not openly beg for alms, as this would bring them within reach of the law; but they just stand and wait, and charitably disposed persons, attracted by their picturesque appearance, and moved to compassion, give them money, ignorant or forgetful of the fact that this money benefits them personally not at all, but the *padrone* whose property they are.

The *padroni* are cruel and pitiless masters, and treat the children just like slaves. If the little ones do not bring home a sufficient sum, they are cruelly beaten and ill-treated, kept without food or nourishment, and sent hungry to bed. Very often these poor children do not get home from their weary rounds till past midnight, and are often found utterly worn out and fast asleep under an archway or on a doorstep.

The effects of this evil system upon its victims are necessarily very bad. They do not go to school, they become very idle, and begin early to drink, smoke, and take to all kinds of vices. They are habitually over-worked and underfed, their staple food being much the same as that to which they are accustomed in their native country, such as maccaroni, rice, and so forth. But the climate is so much more rigorous in England, the fogs of smoky London so different from the warm clear air of sunny Italy, that they cannot live properly on such diet, even if they had enough of it to eat, which is very seldom the case. They suffer especially from the diseases of the throat and pulmonary affec-tions brought on by this underfeeding, and by being exposed to all kinds of weather. The mortality from these causes is, of necessity, considerable. Every year many die. But the lot of those who survive is sadder still. They grow up immoral, illiterate, vicious, and low, a degraded class, exercising the most undesirable influence upon those with whom they come in contact. They are wretchedly lodged, huddled together, four or five sleeping in a bed, when they have one to sleep in at all. Being private houses, their lodgings are not in any way open to inspection. To them the word "home," so sacred to English ears, has no meaning at all, and with them decency, cleanliness and modesty become unimaginable things. Here is a description of a sleeping room—it often serves for a living room as well—in one of the ordinary dwelling houses in the neighbourhood of Saffron Hill. In this one room, neither very lofty nor very large, may frequently be found a dozen persons herded together rather like cattle than human beings, sleeping promiscuously as follows :—In one bed, or what serves for a bed, a married couple ; in the next, two young girls ; in a third, a single young man ; in a fourth, three or four children of different ages and sexes, and so on ! The sanitary arrangements of these dwellings leave everything to be desired, and in the sleeping room referred to, owing to the lack of ventilation, and the number of human beings crowded therein, to quote the words of my informant, "The stench is awful." And yet this particular instance is a fair sample of all the rest !

As a result of this promiscuous intercourse, the girls, especially, nearly all go to the bad. They are entirely at the mercy of the infamous *padrone*, who gets these young and unprotected girls under his baleful influence, and at an age of fourteen, fifteen, or sixteen, seduces them. After that their downward course is certain, and it is rendered easier from the fact that in the exercise of their vagrant calling, they are often sent into low drinking-shops, public-houses, and similar places where bad characters abound. The boys, when they grow up, become beggars by profession, and always remain so, for they learn no other trade, and can neither read nor write. Some remain in England, but many go over to Italy and bring back children themselves. Sometimes, when they are seventeen or eighteen years old, they run away from the *padroni* and set up on their own account.

The *padroni* are men utterly without principle, and morally bad in every way. I will sketch the career of one of them, who is, I believe, not a wit more infamous than many of his fellows. I am not permitted in this instance to give the precise source of my information, but it is absolutely trustworthy.

Guiseppe Delicato, for such is this man's name, is a *padrone*, who for many years has carried on his infamous traffic in Birmingham. His business would seem to be a very extensive one, since, in addition to the establishment at Birmingham, he has also similar houses in Phœnix Street, Plymouth, and Marsh Street, Hanley, for the purpose of plying his trade in those places as well. He is a native of Rosanico Contrado, in the province of Attina, and would seem to be a man of some standing in his native country, since he is well acquainted with Signor Bernardo Mancini, Mayor of Attina, with whom he is in the habit of frequently corresponding in reference to his business matters. Delicato has made frequent journeys to Italy for the purpose of engaging recruits. On several occasions he has brought with him, on his return, girls whom he has subsequently seduced. It is impossible to give a full list of his victims, but in order to show that I do not exaggerate this man's iniquities, I will give a few instances which are well authenticated. One case is that of Marannia Tada, aged twenty, a native of Sora-di-Compigno, in the province of Cersata, who has borne two children by him. A second case is that of a young girl named Macolata Faccinda, of Pisanisco, province of Cersata, by whom he has had another child. Some time since he also seduced an English girl named Annie Tyler, who bore him three children. He afterwards induced an Italian, named Pietro Dibonce, to marry her, and they left England for America in March of this year (1891). Many other young Italian girls have also fallen victims to this man, but as the inquiry into his antecedents is not yet complete, it is not possible at present to give more details. In common with many other *padroni*, Guiseppe Delicato has not confined his traffic only to children. Whole families, mother, father, and children, are brought over to England for the purpose of begging and playing instruments about the streets. Here is an instance of a family imported by him—a father, mother, and two children. They were in Delicato's service for two or three years, carrying on the *Mestiere*, or trade of vagrancy and begging. At the end of that time the record of this unfortunate family was as follows : Delicato paid the father £2 only for three years' work, and discharged him ; the mother he had previously sent back to Italy, as from ill-health she had become practically useless to him ; one of the girls he seduced, who is still living under what, by a cruel misnomer, would be called his "protection," and he refused to pay the other girl's wages because she had married and left him. Her husband has brought an action against him to recover the money. The action is still pending, and since it has been brought, inquiries have been instituted, which have brought to light the iniquities this man has been carrying on for years. These incidents happened in Birmingham.

The parents are often as cruel as the *padroni ;* in fact, considering the relations which ought to exist between them and their children, they are worse. They seem to have no sense of parental responsibilities, and they look upon their children only as means whereby to fill their pockets with money. Although often well able to afford it, they will not even supply their children with boots, and allow them to run about bare-footed in rain and mud, or apply to the Italian Benevolent Society for assistance, representing themselves as being in such a destitute condition that they cannot afford to bay them.

The traffic is most lucrative, and the gains which

the *padroni*, more especially, make out of these children, are very large; so much so, that after a few years they are able to retire to sunny Italy, and to live as *proprietari*, or country gentlemen. Sometimes the children will bring home as much as ten shillings in a day, and as, often, one *padrone* has as many as fifty children under his care, spread about in companies in London and the country, under the supervision of his confederates, it will be seen that the total amount of the number of small sums accumulating daily must be very large. Of course, sometimes the children bring home very little, and sometimes nothing at all, but as the penalty in this case is a beating, and being kept without food, fear stimulates their efforts, and they seldom return empty-handed.

Many efforts have been made to put a stop to this disgraceful traffic. The Italian Benevolent Society, established in London—a Society which might serve as a model for others, both from its admirably organized system of relief, and for the efforts it makes to discourage these people from coming to England— has been especially energetic in the matter. Under its auspices, several petitions have been made to the English Government, one to the Home Secretary, to bring the matter before him with the aid of the Embassy. So long ago as 1877 an inquiry into this question was instituted by the Charity Organization Society, and a deputation waited on the Home

Secretary, then Sir Richard Cross, with the result
that a circular was addressed to the police magistrates,
asking them to help in dealing with these children, so
that where it was possible they should be returned to
Italy. The Italian Benevolent Society can only deal
with the children when they are handed over by the
magistrates. The Society has returned a great many
in this way to Italy, but as a rule they come back
again. If the children are taken from the *padroni*,
the parents often bring them themselves, and then, of
course, they cannot be taken away from their parents.
The only visible effect has been to reduce slightly the
number of *padroni*, and to increase the number of
parents; but, as I have said before, the parents are
so unnatural, that whether the children are brought
here by them or by the *padroni*, the evil effects of
the system remain the same.

In 1876 the Italian Benevolent Society went on a
deputation to the London School Board, and it was
decided to compel these children to go to school in
the same way as if they had been English children,
and an Italian School Board officer was appointed for
the purpose. The consequence was that many were
compelled to go to school, chiefly to the schools
connected with the Roman Catholic Church of St.
Peter, in Hatton Garden, which, with the adjoining
portions of Saffron Hill and New Rosebery Avenue,
forms the principal Italian quarter in London. There,

in stunted streets and in narrow courts choked with
ice-cream barrows, vendors of hot chestnuts, and such-
like delicacies, will be found not only a large colony
of these imported itinerant musicians, but also a
young Italy which has never been further abroad than
the sunny slopes of Clerkenwell Green. But to return
to the action of the School Board. The *padrone* was
equal to the occasion. Leaving his beloved haunts
of Saffron Hill he fled eastward and westward to
the suburbs of Deptford, Greenwich, Kingston and
Hammersmith. The School Boards out of London
take no action in this matter, to compel these children
to go to school, so there his slaves reside, and ply
their trade undisturbed by that terror of indigenous
truants, the School Board officer, and the evil is not
sensibly affected or diminished.

By the recent Children's Protection Act a step has
been made in the right direction, and the state of
affairs slightly ameliorated. In consequence of this
Act, a good many Italian boys under fourteen years of
age, and girls under sixteen, have been taken up for
playing and performing in the public streets, and the
parents or masters punished. This new Act, if only it
were rigorously and universally applied, would be a
great help in checking the evil, but it is not sufficient
to eradicate it altogether, as the limit of age is fixed
rather too low. Signor Righetti, the courteous and
energetic secretary of the Italian Benevolent Society,

to whom I am indebted for much valuable information,
and who has been untiring in his endeavours to check
this traffic, wrote to me in a recent letter: "the state
of affairs is somewhat better on account of this Act,
but not very much."

In Italy, where the evil had attained intolerable
proportions, seriously affecting the social wellbeing
and prosperity of the nation, a very rigorous law was
passed in 1873. The history of this Act is rather a
curious one. Ten years previous to its passing, a
former Italian Ambassador to the Court of St. James',
at that time Secretary to the Embassy, on coming out
from a grand reception at one of the mansions in
Piccadilly, found himself literally surrounded by a
crowd of Italian children, who pestered him for alms,
and impeded his free progress by their importunities.
This incident made such a profound impression upon
him, that he directed his especial attention to the
condition of the Italian colony in London, and with
this result. He was so horrified when he became
aware of the nature and extent of the evil, that his
strong representations to the Italian Government, and
the unceasing efforts which he made to obtain some
legislation for the purpose of checking the system of
mendicancy and vagrancy, which had become a bye-
word and a reproach to his country, were mainly
instrumental in passing the drastic Italian law of
1873. By this Act, whoever hands over to be

employed, or employs persons of either sex under the age of eighteen in the exercise of vagrant professions, such as "jugglers, conjurers, clowns, itinerant players or singers, tight rope dancers, diviners of dreams, exhibitors of animals, mendicants, and such like," is liable to both fine and imprisonment. Italian subjects who employ Italian children in a foreign state in vagrant professions, or who entrust them to others to be so employed, are also liable to the penalties of fine and imprisonment; in case of bad usage and illtreatment, the punishment is three years' imprisonment, and if the children have been entrapped or kidnapped by violence, the penalty is seven years. In Italy this Act has produced most beneficial results, but it does not appear to have in any way lessened the evil traffic in England, where all efforts, legislative or otherwise, have hitherto fallen short of the mark.

Several suggestions have been made by which the existing state of affairs may be remedied, all worthy of consideration. One is to increase the limit of age laid down by the Children's Protection Act to eighteen years of age in the case of persons of both sexes. This would bring the Act still closer in accord with the law of Italy. The limit of age at present fixed by the law is too low, and for this reason. Directly the children leave school, at about fourteen years of age —I speak here of those resident in London, who are under the supervision of the Italian School Board

officer—they are put on to the streets to ply the
mestiere. It is an impressionable age. All the good
they learn at school is quickly undone, and the law is
powerless to touch them, whereas, if the limit of age
were fixed at eighteen, the *mestiere* could not long be
followed, and the parents would provide them with
some definite occupation, or put them to learn some
proper trade, so that their time would not be wasted.

Another suggestion is that there should be a general
tightening of the compulsory method by the School
Boards all over the country. Let the *padrone* know
that in every English town his singing boys and
playing girls will be hurried off to school by the
School Board Officer, he will soon find his gains
decrease. If only the children could be compelled to
live laborious days in school, the occupation of the
padrone would be gone, and his dream of returning to
la bell' Italia, to live there as a country gentleman,
would vanish for ever. It is illogical that the compulsory action of the School Board should be enforced in London, and allowed to remain idle in the
provinces.

The third and most drastic remedy, and by far the
most effective, would be to adopt the American plan,
and stop the children at the ports of arrival when
they come to England, and send them back at once
to their own country; and not the children only, but
the whole class of destitute, idle, and useless immi-

grants who attempt to land upon our shores. Signor Righetti, who has gone into this question of Italian immigration more thoroughly than any one else, is especially emphatic in declaring that this is the only efficacious way in which the evil can be eradicated.

At present, however, we have no laws on the subject of foreign immigration, and though doubtless before long some such restrictions as those recently enforced by the United States Government will have to be adopted here, yet it is idle to deny, having regard to the present state of public business and public feeling, that any legislation of this kind must of necessity be tardy. In the meantime, what is to be done? For a nation which was foremost in abolishing the slave trade to tamely tolerate in its midst an inhuman traffic such as this, is something worse than an anachronism. It is a blot and a reproach upon our vaunted civilization.

The Children's Protection Act is declared to be insufficient to cope with this evil. Very energetic measures are needed against the masters and parents of these poor children. At present the punishment is far too mild. A fine or a few weeks' imprisonment counts as nothing to them in comparison to the gains they make. As an instance of this a magistrate once made a *padrone* deposit £20 with the Italian Benevolent Society as a guarantee that he would take some children back to Italy, but the £20 still remains in

the hands of the Society, and the man did not go,
saying, as he quitted the court, " What is the money
to us? We can soon make it over again!" If a
child is left an orphan there is always a great rush
for it among the *padroni*. They will promise anything, however extravagant, if they think they can
gain possession of it to use it for their own infamous
purposes.

One remedy, at least, can be put into force at once,
and that independently of all legislation. It is simply
for the English public to refrain from giving the
children money. The misplaced generosity of charitable persons is the cause of so many of these little
ones being brought over here to lead a life of degradation and ruin. The public should bear in mind
that neither directly nor indirectly do the children
benefit by the alms so thoughtlessly given. On the
contrary, the money goes to swell the ill-gotten gains
of the parents and *padroni*, and to encourage and
foster a system fraught with evil consequences, not
only to the recipients of their bounty, but to the community at large.

The great thing is to lose no opportunity of bringing this truth before the notice of the public. Some
little time since the *Times*, commenting upon a letter
which I, at the request of the Italian Benevolent
Society, had written for their columns, condemned in
no measured terms this disgraceful traffic. The

matter was taken up warmly by the provincial papers, and by the Press of Italy, and for a time it really seemed that some good might be done. For a time only, and then some new sensation arose, and the iniquities of the *padrone*, and the sufferings of his poor little victims, were thrust aside and forgotten. In fact, instead of the Press using its great influence to stamp out the evil, one portion of it—some of the children's papers—have unwittingly encouraged it. Only the other day I came across, in a paper for children's reading, a picture of an Italian organ-grinder, with an expression of unusual amiability on his swarthy face, and by his side was standing a little child looking up in mute appeal for alms, while underneath the legend ran : " Give something to the pretty little Italian child, who comes from the sunny south, and is so poor, and yet sings happily all the day." A pretty illusion indeed ; but the veriest fable that was ever invented by the imagination of man ! The legend should rather have run : " Have mercy on the poor little Italian child, who comes from the foul dens of Saffron Hill, who is half-starved, cruelly beaten, and robbed of every penny of its earnings, and who sings in mortal terror of the brutal master, who grows rich upon its sufferings."

A good deal of anxious thought has of late been expended on the subject of black slavery in Africa. Would it not be well that some attention should be given to this form of white slavery at home? On a superficial aspect of the life of these youthful vagrants, the idea of slavery is probably the last which would occur to one in connection with them. They are apparently free and listless as the air they breathe, and as lightly tasked as any children in the land. It is only when we come to look beneath the surface, and examine the conditions of this seemingly careless existence, that its cruelty, hardship, and injustice become manifest. I have shown that many succumb to the miseries of their lot, and go down unheeded to an early grave. But what of those who survive, who grow up to manhood and to womanhood amid the contamination of these corrupt surroundings? Is not their lot sadder still? Can nothing be done to rescue these worse than orphans from their life of moral and physical ruin? The problem is not an easy one, I admit, but surely some attempt might be made to solve it, some organized effort on the part of charitable and philanthropic persons, bearing in mind the words of One who made little children His especial care: "Inasmuch as ye have done it unto one of the least of these My brethren, ye have done it unto Me."

FOREIGN PAUPER IMMIGRATION.

By S. H. Jeyes.

"LET the alarmist sleep easy on his bed"—so Mr. Charles Booth declared in the first volume of his "Labour and Life of the People"—"untroubled by visions of Oriental hordes of barbarians, streaming in like Huns and Vandals, and snatching the bread from the mouth of the much-enduring Londoner. Whatever may have been the cause for alarm presented by the immigration of the Jew, it is all over now—at least for the present." These words of reasoned comfort were published in 1889: they could not be repeated in 1891. When Mr. Booth wrote them we had apparently reached the end of a period marked by an abnormal influx of destitute exiles. In 1881 and 1882 a violent if somewhat intermittent persecution had been directed against the Jews in Russia; about two years later an edict was issued by Prince Bismarck, which aimed at expelling the Poles from Prussia. Realizing, as best they could, such poor possessions as they owned, and departing with all possible haste, the expatriated wretches made every attempt to reach a more hospitable land: those who could muster the passage-money were bound for America; the rest, the more destitute and the elderly ones (the great majority

of the exodus), were hoping to settle in the great
English towns. The immediate and permanent result
may be given in Mr. Booth's carefully moderate
language :—

"The newcomers have gradually replaced the English
population in whole districts which were formerly outside
the Jewish quarter. Formerly in Whitechapel, Commercial
Street roughly divided the Jewish haunts of Petticoat Lane
and Goulston Street from the rougher English quarter lying
to the east. Now (1889) the Jews have flowed across this
line ; Hanbury Street, Fashion Street, Pelham Street, Booth
Street, Old Montague Street, and many other streets and
lanes and alleys have fallen before them : they fill whole
blocks of model dwellings ; they have introduced new trades
as well as new habits, and they live and crowd together, and
work and meet their fate almost independent of the great
stream of London life surging round them."

Nor must it be supposed that this is the only Jewish
quarter in the metropolis ; that London is the only
town which the foreigners invade ; or, finally, that
the host of immigrants is exclusively recruited from
the Children of Israel. We have no trustworthy
means of numbering our uninvited visitors, though
various bases of calculation have been suggested. We
may count the Jewish funerals reported to the Jewish
Board of Guardians in a year, and thus form some
approximate estimate of the total Jewish population.
But it is well known that infant mortality constitutes
a large percentage of the death-rate, and there are
but few infants among those immigrants, for reasons

which are sufficiently obvious. Again, we may look
at the returns of Jewish children in the Elementary
Schools, and adopting the method of the Education
Department, multiply by six to find the total colony.
But these Jews are notoriously and unhappily prolific ;
their multiplying capacity cannot be estimated on a
Gentile basis. Finally, we may resort to the Alien
Lists which are supposed to be drawn out by captains
of ships entering the port of London. They are
enjoined by the Alien Act of William IV.—which
is not obsolete, but merely disregarded. " The lists
are still handed in," Mr. Booth says, "and filed at the
Home Office, but they are never checked, and are so
loosely made out that a whole family is often returned
as only one person." Nor can we expect that the
agents and servants of the steamship companies will
go out of their way to call public attention to the
magnitude of a traffic on which they subsist and thrive.
There is no reason to accuse anybody of systematic
evasion or wilful deception ; but we are entitled to
make a very considerable addition to any figures
which might be reached by a study of the Alien Lists,
documents so generally ignored that (although they
have been summarised since 1888 and the results published) on June 22nd a member of Parliament felt
himself justified in asking the Home Secretary
whether the Act under which they were required was
still in existence ! For the present, until they have

been strictly enforced and a return published, we are compelled almost to ignore them and to make our computation, such as it is, upon the other data mentioned by Mr. Booth. Using these he reckoned that in 1889 the Jewish population numbered somewhere between 60,000 and 70,000. He put the gross annual influx between 1881 and 1889 at an average of about 4,000, "falling from about 5,000 or 6,000 in the earlier years, to 2,000 or 3,000 in the later years." From these confessedly rough calculations, Mr. Booth was justified in writing the sentences quoted at the beginning of this article. The alarm, he said, was all over then—*at least for the present.*

He did well to add that final proviso. The tide had not turned, though it seemed for a brief period to be slackening. We were very soon undeceived. Let us turn to the official reports for the following year, the " Statistical Tables relating to Emigration and Immigration from and into the United Kingdom in the year 1890, and report to the Board of Trade thereon." These were published last March, and their accuracy, so far as they go, is attested by the name of Mr. Robert Giffen. Without giving the total number of Jewish immigrants in any year, the following table is confined to those persons who fall under the title of destitute aliens. When they arrived in England, or soon afterwards, they were compelled to ask for assistance from their charitable co-religionists here :—

NUMBER OF APPLICATIONS FOR RELIEF TO THE JEWISH BOARD
OF GUARDIANS, NUMBER OF CASES RELIEVED, AND NUM-
BER OF NEW CASES RELIEVED BY THE BOARD IN EACH OF
THE UNDERMENTIONED YEARS.

Year.	Number of Appli- cations for Relief (Cases).	Number of Cases Relieved.	Number of New Cases only.
1876 . . .	1,903	1,851	606 [1]
1877 . . .	2,296	2,242	862 [1]
1878 . . .	2,471	2,410	873 [1]
1879 . . .	2,639	2,557	1,003 [1]
1880 . . .	2,553	2,441	945 [1]
1881 . . .	2,629	2,350	984 [1]
1882 . . .	2,953	2,775	1,306 [1]
1883 . . .	2,882	2,737	1,103 [1]
1884 . . .	3,313	3,054	1,368
1885 . . .	3,596	3,408	1,536
1886 . . .	4,497	4,139	1,944
1887 . . .	3,415	3,313	1,205
1888 . . .	3,719	3,513	1,318
1889 . . .	3.131	2,980	923
1890 . . .	3,569	3,351	1,319

But these figures are even more formidable than
they appear to be. No statement is made on the
point; but we are reasonably entitled to assume that
a very great proportion, and perhaps a majority, of
these "Applications for Relief" stand, not for so
many individuals, but for so many families—perhaps
large families. It has already been hinted that the
plague or (shall we say?) the embarrassment caused
by these destitute aliens is not confined to London.

[1] Up to 1883 the figures in this column include cases refused as
well as cases relieved, but the numbers are small.

Just to bring out this very important, but often ignored, part of the problem, it may be useful to quote the case of Manchester :—

STATISTICS OF RELIEF BY THE MANCHESTER JEWISH BOARD OF GUARDIANS IN EACH OF THE UNDERMENTIONED YEARS.

Compiled from the Report of the Manchester Jewish Board of Guardians.

	1889–90.	1888–89.	1887–88.
Number of applicants . .	865 [1]	843 [2]	1,109
Number of applications .	1,085 [1]	1,094 [2]	1,387
Applications refused . .	95	142	178
Relieved :—			
Residents	888 [1]	756 [2]	995
Casuals	183	196	219
Fixed weekly cases . .	372	396	389
TOTAL . . .	1,443 [1]	1,348 [2]	1,603
Number of times relieved .	4,511 [1]	4,365 [2]	4,706

It has already been explained why the Alien Lists cannot be accepted as containing any near approach to the actual numbers of foreigners landing at the port of London. Yet, in Mr. Giffen's words, they show "a notable increase," especially as regards arrivals from Hamburg, the point from which most

---

[1] To compare 1889–90, when holidays occurred in April, September, and October, with 1888–89, when holidays occurred only in September, and no Passover relief was given—Passover having occurred twice during the financial year 1887–88—deduct 70.

[2] To compare 1888–89 with 1887–88, add 170.

of the superfluous Jews of the Continent are passed on to the United Kingdom, or perhaps to America—no matter which, so long as they do not stay on the European Continent. The number of aliens entered in these Lists (where one person's name frequently stands for those of a whole family, *teste* Mr. Charles Booth), rose from 9,846 in 1889 to 11,262 in 1890—an increase of 4,416. It is not, however, to foreigners as such that we make objection, but to those of them who are destitute or on the verge of destitution. For these we must particularly look to the immigrants from Hamburg. And we find with less surprise than concern that the number of arrivals from this port alone rose from 5,978 in 1889 to 9,834 in 1890—an increase of 3,856. Not all are destitute, not all stay with us; but those who go away are just those whom, if we had to choose, we should prefer to remain : those with some money in their pockets, some vigour in their bodies, some enterprise in their hearts. The Continent shoots its outcasts on these devoted islands : they are sifted here by natural selection : and we keep the refuse.

According to the Chief Commissioner of the Metropolitan Police, by one line which trades between Hamburg and London, no less than 4,000 aliens were landed here last year, of whom *eighty per cent. appeared to be quite destitute* ; the total *additional* number of such immigrants was from 4,000 to 5,000 ; and, although some were merely passing through London on their way to America, the *majority* came to settle here. The Chief Constable at Manchester reports that of the 15,000 or 16,000 Jews in that city not less than seventy per cent. are believed to be Russian Poles, and that the Jewish population there has very largely increased during the last few years. The Chief Constable at Leeds, on the authority of the local Jewish Board of Guardians, says that the number of Jewish immigrants arriving at that town last year was about 2,000, this being an increase of a few hundreds.

But before we part with the report from Leeds, we must quote a particularly enlightening passage. The authorities referred to, it is declared, know of no society in Leeds to assist alien immigration, but—

"A firm of money lenders state that they lend money to Jewish applicants for any purpose, but, in many cases, there are applicants who express a desire to send for their friends or relations from Russia or Poland when they obtain the money; but their society is not established for any such purpose; they lend money to any one who finds the necessary security."

Here we come upon a clue to the puzzle how it is that destitute aliens find the means to pay their passage money to England. And connected with this is the system of charitable relief established by the Jewish Boards of Guardians (some of whose work is purely beneficent, that part, at least, which consists

in sending back to their own countries those new-
comers who could not pick up a living here, and in
passing others on to America), and by the Poor Jews'
Temporary Shelter (whose philanthropic activity sometimes assumes a more questionable shape), and, in
principle the worst of all, by the London Society for
Promoting Christianity amongst the Jews. Of the
last-named institution Miss Beatrice Potter has given
a dryly humorous account. It enjoys, she says, an
income of £35,000 a year; it is housed in magnificent
premises, comprising a chapel, a missionary training
institute, and an operatives' home. In the year 1888
it baptized twelve Jews in the chapel, maintained
forty children in the school, and supported twelve
converts in the home. "The process of conversion
is very simple; board and lodging at a specially furnished house during the inquiry stage, constant charitable assistance after conversion, and free education
and free maintenance of Jewish children brought up
in the Christian faith. . . . Imagine the temptа-
tion to the poverty-stricken inhabitants of the crowded
alleys of the Jewish slum." But the infinitesimal per-
formances of this Gentile society might be left out of
account for the present purpose, were they not known
to have aroused an unhealthy emulation among the
charitable Jews. Determined to protect the friend-
less, destitute, unemployed immigrant from these the
material allurements of Christian enterprise, they set

up a rival institution in the above-mentioned Poor
Jews' Temporary Shelter, which has fallen into considerable disfavour, even in the community to which
it belongs, because, rightly or wrongly, it is believed
to attract pauper immigrants to this country. Nor
could we be surprised if such were the case, since in
1883 it " provided board and lodging for a period of
from one to fourteen days to 1,322 homeless immigrants."

The mischievous effect of these charitable agencies
(which have been reduced to the practicable *minimum*,
it should be admitted, in the case of the Jewish Boards
of Guardians) is not greatly counteracted by the
official warnings which are issued by our Consuls
abroad. Against them have to be set the undeniable
chances of making some sort of a living here; the
certainty of complete political liberty and religious
toleration; escape from the conscription; the generous assistance of their co-religionists; and—last but
not least—the blandishments of the agents of the
German shipping companies. The British vessels
engaged in this traffic—so we are informed in the
report of our Acting Consul-General at Hamburg—
only carry the *bonâ fide* emigrants, that is, those who
have obtained through tickets to the United States
or other parts. But the German vessels are under no
such restrictions. The question is how long we shall
wink at a traffic which we could stop by a short and

N

simple Act of Parliament. At present we seem to confine ourselves to publishing, in certain foreign newspapers, circulating among the class from which the emigrants are taken, notices such as the following, in German, Hebrew, and English :

"Her Britannic Majesty's Consul-General at —— has been instructed to cause it to be made public that destitute persons intending to emigrate to Great Britain to seek employment are likely to be disappointed on arrival, the prospects of obtaining employment being very limited."

Destitute persons ! But who is destitute if he has friends abroad who will lend him passage-money, and a society which gives him temporary board and lodging, starts him in a humble way of business, and, at the very worst, pays his passage back again to the place whence he came ?

This question of Alien Immigration came to the front in England when the news was confirmed that the Czar had at last hardened his heart to publish and enforce those edicts against his Russian subjects which had long been lying in his desk—edicts which he had allowed to remain dormant, perhaps through the fear of enraging (as he has enraged) the cosmopolitan Jewish millionaires, who can make a loan or mar it (they chose to mar the last) ; perhaps through some remaining sense of duty or spark of pity towards subjects who have as full a right to his care and protection as any Slav in his dominions. But policy and religious zeal—the policy of keeping Russia for the Russians, the zeal of bigotry—have at last prevailed; and a series of rules and regulations are being remorselessly exercised against the daily life of the Jews, their religion, their traditions, their ways of subsistence, which amount in effect to a general decree of exile. Nominally restrictive, they are really expulsory, and five million Jews are looking out for a home. There are plenty of reasons why they should turn to England as the land of their choice. They will not come at once : to mobilize an army of one-fifth of that number, consisting of able-bodied men, and without regard for expenditure, is a feat of organization which would puzzle a great captain. These expatriated Jews can only pass over in driblets. But the important and the dangerous thing for us is that the process has unmistakably commenced, and is going on none the less steadily because the beginning was slow.

There is no doubt that these aliens are swarming upon the Port of London ; no doubt that the majority will remain amongst us ; no doubt, unhappily, that they are practically paupers.

The opinion that we should impose some legislative restriction upon the free immigration of destitute aliens is naturally strongest among the working classes of the great towns, who find the rate of wages for Unskilled Labour sensibly reduced by the compe-

tition of foreigners more frugal and certainly more
sober than themselves. On the face of it, that is a
selfish and almost an ignoble motive. But we must
remember, in the first place, that we have made the
working-men our masters, and that through their
parliamentary representatives, whom they are able to
treat as mere delegates, they have the power of giving
effect to their views. Already we find that a considerable number of Members of Parliament, *in esse*
and *in posse*, are prepared to vote for regulations here
such as are in force in Germany and the United
States. Amongst them are men who are above the
suspicion of mere popularity-hunting, and who have
achieved a certain position in politics, such as Mr.
Darling, Q.C., M.P. for Deptford, and Mr. R. G.
Webster, M.P. for East St. Pancras, and Mr. L. J.
Jennings, M.P. for Stockport—not to mention Lord
Dunraven, who has no votes to court. In the present
demoralized state of politics it is easy to suggest
doubts about this man's honesty and that man's ear-
nestness; we are not concerned, however, with the
inner workings of the parliamentary conscience, but
with the reasons which underlie what is certainly a
powerful sentiment in many populous constituencies.
To begin with, the dislike for alien competition is not
purely selfish : it proceeds not from individual avarice,
but a feeling of corporate loyalty. Englishmen who belong to the same trade have a notion that they ought to

stand by one another in the interests of all ; they despise those whom they regard as traitors to the common
cause. That is why, in a strike, decent and generally
amiable men will bully and maltreat the "blacklegs"
and the "knobsticks" and the "scallywags." The
motive does not justify, but it does explain, conduct
which ought to be vigilantly exposed and sternly
punished by law. Now these resident aliens in London are the "blacklegs" and the "knobsticks" and
the "scallywags" of the Unskilled Labour market.
They will do more work for less wages than their
English rivals ; they submit without grumbling to the
petty tyrannies of the overseer and the mean exac-
tions of the sweater ; they join no Trade Union ; many
of them, perhaps most, do not speak English, and
they mix very little with Englishmen ; they marry
and give in marriage amongst their own people ; in
their virtues as in their vices they are a race apart.
Under no circumstances would they be popular here ;
but since they succeed, if not in taking the bread out
of English mouths, at least in reducing the margin of
wages which might be spent on beer and gin, they are
naturally and not quite unfairly detested. In fine,
they are believed, rightly or wrongly, to be responsible for that bundle of abuses and misfortunes which
are lumped together under the name of the Sweating
System.

If we are ever to abolish or modify that system, we

must control, not the much-abused Sweater, but his
much-pitied victims the sweated workers. The sweater
is generally an industrious and often a decent fellow ;
he takes his share in the job that is going on in his
place, supervising and stimulating, sometimes with
encouragement and sometimes with curses. His
functions are to find out trustworthy workmen and
keep them up to the mark—a business which must
be learned and practised by somebody. If it were
not done under the sub-contract or " sweating" system, it would have to be undertaken by paid agents of
the great trading houses, and there is nothing to show
that it would be carried out with more humanity or
greater generosity. Let us look the facts in the face
and admit that every producer who is working for a
profit in days of free and open competition is bound
to cut down expenses to the lowest possible figure.
Turn and twist the principle how we may, this comes
to grinding the faces of the poor. We should not
eradicate or even mitigate the practice by abolishing
the middleman or " sweater," and replacing him by
the paid agent or departmental supervisor employed
by the principal. The money now taken as the
middleman's profits would then be absorbed in the
supervisor's salary and percentage. No, if we wish to
see better wages paid, we must go to the workman
direct, and induce him to insist on a more adequate
remuneration. To such an exhortation English work-

men give a ready and, perhaps, too ready response; but these pauper, or nearly pauper, aliens are deaf to it. Our own countrymen have a higher standard of comfort; rather than accept wages which fall below it they will go on strike, if they have a Union at their backs; and, if they have not, they will resort to the workhouse or, more likely, pick up a precarious but not fatiguing livelihood as corner-men, street-loafers, cas'lty labourers or occasional criminals. It is because the pauper aliens prefer to go on working for a regular pittance (and even save money on it, so penurious are their habits) that they reduce the rate of wages in the Unskilled Labour market, and, in fact, make possible the Sweating System which we all deplore.

It would be impossible here to cover the vast and rather shifting topics discussed in the evidence and report of the Lords' Committee on the Sweating System. But one or two points may be touched upon. Mr. Arnold White made the remarkable statement that *if there were no poor foreigners there would be no sweating system*—a statement which he subsequently modified and confined to the special case of the boot-making trade. The original statement was, of course, too broad; we must take account, not only of the poor foreigners, but also of the poor Englishwomen, whose competition with male labour has a lowering tendency on the general rate of wages. But it is

certain that, if we could remove "the greeners" from
the slums of our great towns, we should unfailingly
strike at one of the two taproots of the Sweating
System. And our own women, under the tutelage of
agitators and philanthropists, would very soon learn
the useful and necessary, if occasionally inconvenient,
lesson how to start and carry on a strike for better
wages. The principle of human advancement is
"progressive desire"—that is, the amiable side of
incessant discontent. At present our underpaid
women are too sensible to refuse work at the current
rate of wages. The money would go to the "greener,"
and they would be so much the worse off. But take
away the "greener," and they would very soon form
Trade Unions, and extort more reasonable wages.
It is said on behalf of the "greener" that he does
not absorb the money hitherto earned by English
persons, but introduces new trades, and accepts work
which our own countrymen reject. That is true to
some extent: the lower branches of tailoring and boot-
making are almost his specialities. But what is the
result? That the better work of our own countrymen is beaten out of the field. In the mania for
cheapness which has demoralized many branches of
English industry, people look to the outward form of
an article, not to its genuine qualities. A coat is a
coat if it covers a back, and a pair of boots is a pair
of boots if they will go on the feet.

Some of the most moderate, least prejudiced, and most trustworthy evidence taken before the Sweating Committee was given by Dr. Billing, now Bishop of Bedford, but then Rector of Spitalfields. He declared that, within his immediate observation of East London, the "greeners" have "very largely displaced native labour," and that under stress of the competition our own people are being driven into pauperism, casual labour, or emigration; that Jews and Gentiles "very seldom work together" (a point in which he was to some degree contradicted by the evidence of Doctor Adler, the late Chief Rabbi); that during the past few years (here confirming Mr. Charles Booth's statement already quoted) whole streets had become entirely populated by foreign Jews "where there was not a Jew before"; that many of those who, having come in search of work and failed to find it, had been charitably assisted home, only returned a second time; and, finally, that he was prepared to refuse to admit by the law of England men flying from persecution abroad. "They are flying," he said, "from one great evil to another, and producing an intolerable evil here." As a rule, it should be admitted that these foreign Jews do not become a direct charge upon the Poor Rates. But they drive our own people into the workhouse or, still worse, into vagabondage; so that in giving asylum to them we are turning Englishmen out of their own homes. It is pretty to talk about our national hospitality, but are we prepared to practise it on these terms? Will the working classes permit us to continue it at such a sacrifice?

There is no proposal to exclude here, as the United States exclude, persons who come under contract of labour; though it might hereafter be advisable thus to extend our legislation if we found that it was being violated by colourable evasions and bogus engagements. At present it will be sufficient to turn back all immigrants without visible means of subsistence, and to send them away in the vessel which had attempted to land them—thus throwing the expense on the persons responsible for the mischief. In the United States a money penalty and a term of imprisonment are further provided to meet the case of any captain or agent who succeeds in unlawfully landing a contraband human cargo, and some such provision would, perhaps, have to be adopted here. But it would not be necessary, in all probability, to make it here, as in the United States, a punishable offence to solicit or encourage immigration. We should probably effect our object—English officials as a rule not being venal—if we made the business risky at all times, and generally futile.

The provisions of the United States Act of 1885 were mainly directed against the unrestricted immigration of Chinese cheap labour. And this brings us to an incidental diplomatic advantage which we should secure by adopting similar legislation. It is well known that one of the points wherein we are not quite at harmony with the Australian colonists is as to the feasibility of regulating Chinese immigration. The colonists insist upon doing so; and it may some day become so urgent a domestic question with them that we shall have to concede them an unlimited discretion. This will be highly offensive at Pekin, and we have the strongest Imperial reasons for wishing to remain on cordial terms with China — the great Eastern counterpoise of Russia and the not unconcerned spectator of her ambitions in Asia. The sting of our refusal to permit Chinese immigration into Australia would be taken away if we could show that restrictions imposed on a particular nation in a particular quarter of the globe were but part of a general Imperial policy—a policy so like the Chinese tradition of exclusiveness that it would not lie in the mouth of Pekin statesmen to protest against it. True, they might retort, if they cared for a barren dialectical triumph, by threatening altogether to close China against British capital and British enterprise. But they will exclude or admit our merchants and engineers according as they want or do not want them. We shall enter when our presence is required; not a day sooner, not a day later.

It has been said that "every nation has the Jew whom it deserves." We have, then, our native English Jews—a better, a sturdier stock, a more desirable body of fellow-citizens, it would not be easy to find. They have their faults, but they are English to the core. In patriotism they are not inferior to any of us Gentiles. But the Jews who are coming to us from Russia and Poland have all the vices which are generated by many centuries of systematic oppression varied with occasional outbursts of violent persecution. It is absurd, of course, to pretend that the morals of our East End will be corrupted by Oriental vices. In the first place, the Jews there do not mix freely with the Gentiles; in the second place, they will compare favourably in many respects with our native countrymen. But—such as they are or have been made—they are politically unfit to be suddenly transplanted into those democratic institutions for which we have adapted ourselves, or partially adapted ourselves, by a long course of self-governing liberty. Their advent might be welcomed, or at least tolerated, if the qualities which they brought were such as would reinforce the weakened fibres of our own town-bred population. If they were a martial race, we might be glad of them. If their tastes and gifts lay towards pastoral and agricultural pursuits, we could find a place for them or their children in the depopulated villages. If the same penurious content and the same untiring industry which they show in the slopshops and sweating-dens were devoted to the work of farm

labourers—which must always be underpaid, and
therefore unattractive to Englishmen, so long as we
import cheap corn—we might utilise the new strain
of blood. But the foreign Jews do not come to man
our Army and Navy (many of them have fled to avoid
the conscription at home); they do not come to till
the soil (they never keep to farm work if they can find
the meanest opening in trade); they come simply to
swell the swollen tide of immigration into the towns,
to reduce the rate of wages there, and therefore to
strengthen that spirit of discontent and disorder on
which the agitators live and batten, and which in
time may pollute the ancient constitutional liberalism
of England with the visionary violence of Continental
Socialism. That would be a disaster not to this or
that party, but to the whole nation. At present it
has not seriously shown itself, for the very good
reason that the foreigners as a body take little part
in our public life. But it would be seen and felt as
soon as they began to amalgamate with our own
people : it is certain that any measure of success
which might be obtained in Anglicising these resident
aliens would be badly compensated by the concurrent
process of Continentalising the native Englishmen.

One word more. It is frequently asserted that the
immigration into England is roughly balanced by the
emigration. That is partially true. But it is not
true (as is shown by the official reports of the Police

Commissioners, and as is known by all who have any thorough acquaintance with the slums of our great towns) that anything approaching such a balance is struck amongst the aliens who come to our great ports. Perhaps the majority, and certainly one-half, come to stay with us. And the emigration lists are swollen with the names of Englishmen prevented from making a worthy living in their own land. We are turning away the pluckiest, the most enterprising, the most valuable of our ordinary workmen, in order to find room for the least progressive and the least desirable natives of other countries. We are exchanging the pick of our manual workmen for the residuum of foreign states. Most of us are vain enough to think that Englishmen are worth retaining at home ; that England should be kept for Englishmen, and the British Empire for the British people. Let the politicians look to this question. The agitators have taken it up : the strike-leaders are discussing it. At present it is a manageable problem ; but if it were neglected much longer, we may witness in civilized England scenes not greatly unlike those outbursts of popular persecution which have recently shocked us in the Ionian Islands—followed, at no distant date, by summary measures of similar aim with those now adopted by the Russian Government. That would not be so much a disgrace to our civilization as a reproach to our short-sighted legislators. If we would go on doing our duty by those aliens whom we have too freely admitted to our citizenship, we must prevent them from growing into a body at once more noxious and more disliked than they are at present. Mr. Burns and Mr. Tillett and Mr. Mann could raise a Judenhetze to-morrow if they liked to do it. It is for the prudent statesman to cut away the ground under their feet. We cannot go on keeping open house for the paupers of all the world.

[Reprinted by permission from the *Fortnightly Review* of July, 1891.]

www.ingramcontent.com/pod-product-compliance
Lightning Source LLC
Chambersburg PA
CBHW030835270326
41928CB00007B/1060